TEACHER'S GOLD MINE II

*By Dorothy Michener
and Beverly Muschlitz*

Incentive Publications, Inc.
Nashville, Tennessee

Cover by Geoffrey Brittingham
Illustrated by Beverly Muschlitz
Edited by Jan Keeling

ISBN 0-86530-150-6

Table of Contents

Preface

Teacher's Gold Mine has been in the marketplace for twelve years, and we think it's still full of good ideas. You, the teachers, have shown us that it has aged well.

However, as is true of most good things, it is now time to "spruce up"—to streamline, and to change with the times.

We have come up with new activities and ideas, but our theme is still the same: Learning *can* be exciting, and fun! Our motto has always been "Success builds success!"

This book deals with specific areas of the curriculum, and the ideas are limitless. Most activities can be used for several grade levels and are adaptable to a "multi-disciplinary" approach.

For example, some worksheets look very difficult. The teacher—or a good reader—can read and explain those materials to the class and help them with the activities. A primary activity does not necessarily have to *look* "child-like."

On the other hand, some of the easier activities can be used on an individual basis with your slow learners. Check out *everything!*

Motivating students is one of the biggest challenges teachers face. In this book we have tried to help with this problem by providing an imaginative format, provocative illustrations, and timely themes. We openly deal with feelings and emotions, urging pupils to share and discuss their problems. Trust is important when using some of these pages.

A good school/home relationship is crucial, and we constantly urge students to take their work home to show, discuss, and share. This involvement will help extend your classroom and further enrich the lives of the children. Create parent-teacher partnerships!

Some of the pages in this book are to be used individually, while others provide an opportunity for "cooperative learning." Students learn from one another. Basic skills and social concerns are enhanced when pupils interact with each other. Provide time for group work, peer teaching, and one-to-one relationships.

Each chapter of **Teacher's Gold Mine II** focuses on a curriculum area or process. Specific instructions are given in each of the introductions. We hope you will find this book helpful and easy to use.

We've not spent a great deal of time telling you "how" to do things, as teachers are known to be clever. When you don't have the materials or resources suggested—improvise. (If you don't have the recommended bottle caps—scrounge, or use buttons or washers.)

Adapt and/or adopt our ideas whenever you can, for they must fit your unique classroom and your style of teaching. Keep in mind the uniqueness of each student.

Once again, we've enjoyed putting together our ideas. Now that **Teacher's Gold Mine II** is complete, our enthusiasm still runs high. We hope you enjoy this book—we'll be back!

Chapter 1

STRIKE GOLD AT

In this chapter we provide a smattering of topics and ideas. We touch on "social ways" and special social studies days, geography, patriotism, universal understanding, and far-flung topics of general interest.

We hope these pages will enhance the daily work you do to teach your social studies curriculum. Most of the pages are self-contained, but many encourage the student to "dig for more." Research is suggested and can usually be achieved at home, the library, at school, or in the community.

A visit to a senior center or nursing home is an excellent way to demonstrate "thinking of others" and "reaching out," important concepts we've stressed in these pages. You may want to start an "adopt a grandparent" program in your classroom.

The world of today has diminished in some ways due to the opportunities of travel, but its challenges have increased geometrically. "Global understanding" is a theme that is essential to present at all levels.

Exposure to the complex world in which we live can be an exciting adventure for today's young people. Open the doors!

STRIKE GOLD AT HOME, AT SCHOOL, IN THE COMMUNITY, AND IN THE WORLD
(Social Studies)

wave the flag

THE MOST IMPORTANT SYMBOL OF A COUNTRY IS ITS FLAG

We show respect for our country's flag in many ways. Check off the things you know.

_____ 1. The flag should be flown only from sunrise to sunset.

_____ 2. The flag can be flown at night only if a spotlight is shining on it.

_____ 3. The flag should be kept clean.

_____ 4. We should never use the flag as a tablecloth or put things on top of it.

_____ 5. The flag should never touch the ground.

_____ 6. When a flag is old we do not throw it away. It can be burned or destroyed by an adult.

_____ 7. There is a right way to fold a flag. Find out the right way and practice it.

Write The Pledge Of Allegiance

_____

_____

_____

_____

_____

NAME _____

Fickle Fashion

Young people can be choosy when it comes to fashion. Do you keep up with the latest fashion fads?

Think about the things that influence the way you dress. Number them in order of importance, with "1" being "most important," and "6" being "least important."

Cost? _____

Friends? _____

Trends? _____

Parents? _____

Comfort? _____

Other? _____

Look in a magazine or catalog for a picture of an article of clothing you would like to have. Paste it here!

How important is keeping up with fashion? Why? _____

_____

_____

Share your thoughts with a friend. Do you have differences?

SHORE THINGS   DESERT STUFF

Many areas of our country and world are **unique.** Look up this word and write its meaning.

Unique means _____
_____

Shore Words and Desert Words
Boat – Prairie Dog – Sail – Rattlesnake – Fish – Coyote – Shell –
Salt Water – Tumbleweed – Dock – Lighthouse – Canyon – Pass – Crab

Select a word to write under each picture.

_____ _____ _____ _____

_____ _____ _____ _____

Use these boxes to show some things that are unique to your area

_____ _____ _____ _____

Special Gift

Special Times Deserve Special Ways

Dig into your pocket. It's time to
buy a gift for someone you love. But
wait—maybe you can think of something better.
What about a "service certificate"? It won't cost you
money, yet it may be appreciated more than something you
would buy in a store. Think about things you can do. Give a gift of love!

- Wash a car
- Babysit
- Clean the house
- Wash windows
- Mow the lawn

- Prepare a meal
- Weed the garden
- ? _____
- ? _____
- ? _____

```
SPECIAL GIFT CERTIFICATE
TO_____
FOR_____
BECAUSE_____

_____        _____
SIGNATURE                     DATE
```

GOLD RUSH BANK

The Gold Rush Bank is a bit short of cash right now. What about you?

Whether you help others decide what to buy, or make purchases yourself, YOU are a consumer! How well do you manage your money?

Use this chart to make a budget plan.

	Week 1	Week 2
Cash I expect:	$ _____	$ _____
Expenses:		
Lunches	_____	_____
Snacks	_____	_____
Movies	_____	_____
Supplies	_____	_____
? _____	_____	_____
? _____	_____	_____
? _____	_____	_____
? _____	_____	_____
? _____	_____	_____

To Think About: Were you able to save money? How well did you plan? Did you do better the second week?

To Do:
Use the space on the back of this page to write about **YOUR** money management.

feasts, festivals, and holidays

Most cultures have celebrations that are a special part of their traditions.

THREE KINGS DAY is celebrated by many Spanish-speaking people on January 5th. This holiday honors the three Kings that brought gifts when Jesus was born.

HANUKKAH is known as the Festival Of Lights and lasts eight days in December. At this time Jewish people celebrate their victory of religious freedom which took place some two thousand years ago.

CHINESE NEW YEAR is a happy festival observed by young and old. This celebration lasts fifteen days and ends with a colorful parade.

TO DO: Write about a special holiday or festival that your family observes. You may want to find out more about a celebration your grandparents had, or about a celebration that belongs to another culture. It would help to find out:

1. Why and when the celebration was held.
2. How long it lasted.
3. Who were invited.
4. What they ate, wore and did.

Begin your report here, then continue on the back of this page. Draw a symbol of this holiday in the space provided.

_____

_____

_____

_____

_____

NAME

FIND YOUR WAY

Streets Near Mine

Pretend you are lost.
How will you get home?
Write the names of the
streets in your
neighborhood on the list.

_____

_____

_____

_____

Draw a map below showing the way you go home from school.

NAME _____

the Green Lady

For more than a hundred years the Statue of Liberty has stood on Liberty Island in New York Harbor. To arriving visitors she has been a symbol of freedom and opportunity offered in the United States.

The copper statue was a gift from France, given as a remembrance of American independence. It was dedicated by President Grover Cleveland on October 28, 1886.

The giant statue wears a crown with seven spokes. At her feet lie the broken bonds of slavery. Her outstretched right hand holds a torch, while the left arm carries a lawbook dated July 4, 1776. Years of weathering have kept the figure a rich, green color.

Millions of immigrants, searching for new lives and new opportunities, have sailed past the impressive lady. The statue is now a national monument, and her torch still burns high.

DO THIS: Read the paragraphs above, then circle five words from the paragraphs that you find in the word maze.

MORE: Find out if you have family members who have arrived from another country. Use the back of this sheet to write about them.

S	B	H	R	K
L	L	A	D	Y
A	I	R	Z	F
V	B	B	N	G
E	E	O	P	R
R	R	R	E	E
Y	T	J	Q	E
C	Y	D	S	N

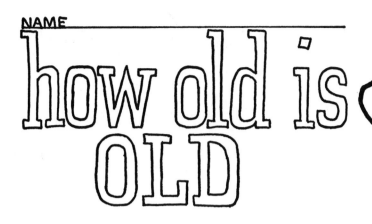

how old is OLD

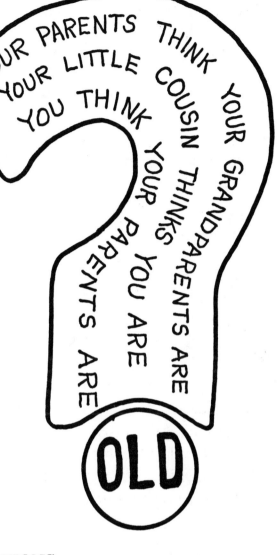

YOUR PARENTS THINK
YOUR LITTLE COUSIN
YOU THINK
YOUR GRANDPARENTS ARE
YOUR PARENTS THINK
YOUR PARENTS ARE
YOU ARE
YOUR PARENTS ARE

OLD

An elderly person is one who has lived many, many years. Some elderly people don't *feel* "old." How old is old?

DO THIS:
Write a report about an elderly person. You may write about a family member, neighbor, or a person you meet during a visit to a retirement or nursing home. Get to know that person. Use this page to take notes for your report. Use the back for more information.

INTERVIEW SUGGESTIONS

Where and when were you born? _____

Describe your family. _____

_____

What was your home like? _____

What was your school like? _____

What kind of work did your parents do? _____

_____

What do you like to do now? _____

_____

WORLD OF PEOPLE

We Share Our World With Many Different Kinds Of People From Other Cultures And Backgrounds

Cut out the "people patterns." Find someone at school or in your neighborhood who is different from you.

DO THIS:

Write words that describe one of you on the back of each pattern. On the fronts, draw yourself and your chosen person.

OUR TOWN

NAME _____

Use the spaces shown to write a travel brochure about your town. After you have all this information, you may want to copy it onto a large, folded sheet of paper, using both sides. Include things that would make people want to visit "Our Town."

PLACES TO VISIT

YEARLY EVENTS

PLACES TO STAY

IMPORTANT FACTS

Population?

Location?

When Founded?

Industry?

Weather?

History?

Descriptive Writing
©1992 by Incentive Publications, Inc., Nashville, TN

Across the CONTINENT or SEA

Settlers from all over the world have come to this country. These people are called immigrants.

Do some research on your family or on a friend's family. How many people in the family came from another country? Make a list of their names and where they came from. Show the total number of immigrants as a circle graph on the globe.

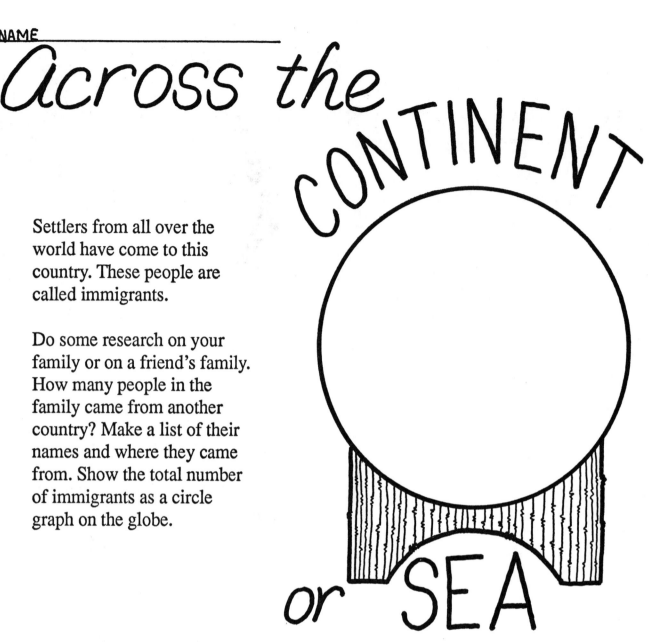

	NAME	FROM
1.	_____	_____
2.	_____	_____
3.	_____	_____
4.	_____	_____
5.	_____	_____
6.	_____	_____
7.	_____	_____
8.	_____	_____

GOAL SETTING

Goals are important. They help us plan for the future. Setting goals helps us to think about, then work for, the things we want in life.

Think about the things you hope will happen this year.
What about:
Grades?
Friends?
Family?
Health?
Appearance?
Activities?
Finances?

Your teacher will return this sheet to you mid-year (January) for a "checkup." See how you are doing.

At the end of the school year (June) — **WOW!**

Goals For _____
(your name)

How Are You Doing?
January   June

1. _____

2. _____

3. _____

4. _____

5. _____

6. _____

7. _____

8. _____

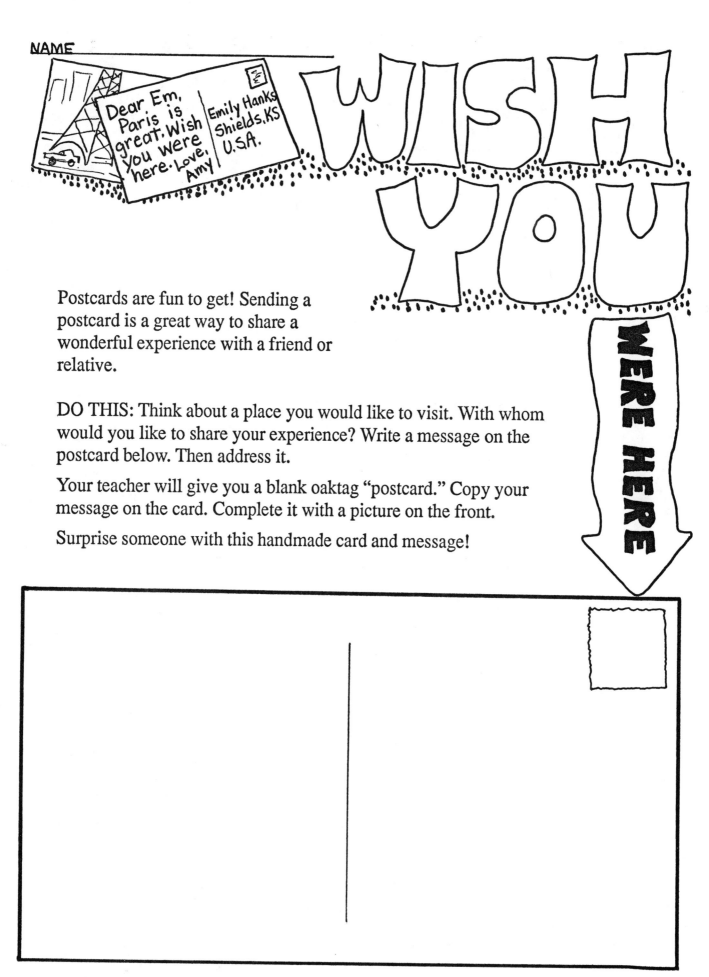

WISH YOU WERE HERE

Dear Em,
Paris is great. Wish you were here. Love, Amy

Emily Hanks
Shields, KS
U.S.A.

Postcards are fun to get! Sending a postcard is a great way to share a wonderful experience with a friend or relative.

DO THIS: Think about a place you would like to visit. With whom would you like to share your experience? Write a message on the postcard below. Then address it.

Your teacher will give you a blank oaktag "postcard." Copy your message on the card. Complete it with a picture on the front.

Surprise someone with this handmade card and message!

NAME

on the road to

Get Out The Maps! Full Speed Ahead With Plans— You Are Going On A Trip!

Use this space to write the names of places you would like to visit.

Places I'd Like To Go!

- Who will I take?

Things I'd Like To Do!

- When will I go?

- How long will I stay?

- How will we travel?

Use this page to think and make notes, then do some research. Make a report that will include drawings, pictures, brochures, and maps. "The sky is the limit" for this imaginary trip.

- What will I need to bring?

- Places to get information . . .

Have A Good Time!

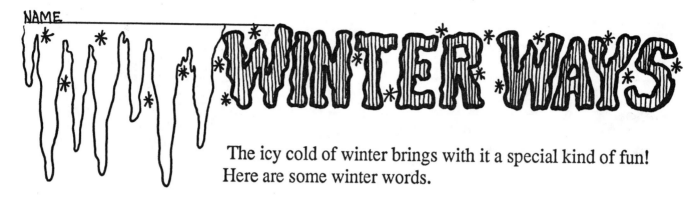

WINTER WAYS

The icy cold of winter brings with it a special kind of fun! Here are some winter words.

Mittens — Snowman — Icicle — Ice Skates — Sled — Boots — Snowflake — Hot Chocolate — Ice — Cold — Toboggan

_____   _____   _____

_____   _____   _____

Write a sentence using each of the words pictured above.

1. _____

2. _____

3. _____

4. _____

5. _____

6. _____

NAME _____

SPRING THINGS

**Spring Is A
Special Time Of Year!**

DO THIS: Color each
picture. Cut each one out.
Look at the list of words.
Add more spring words.
Find the words that best
describe each picture.
Write those words on the
back of each shape.

Yellow
Soft
Fur
Hop
Hoof
Down
Wool
Smell
Petal
Baa
Curly
Peep
Whiskers
Leaves
Ears
Pretty
Tail
Feathers
Fuzzy

_____
_____
_____
_____

NAME _____

THE SHAPE OF FALL

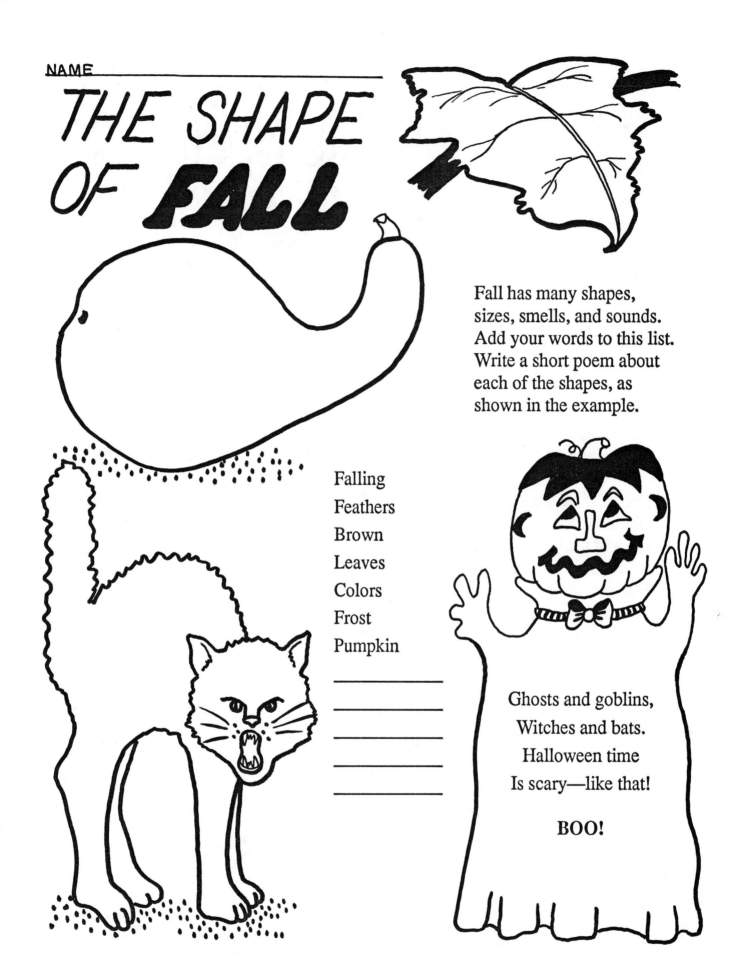

Fall has many shapes, sizes, smells, and sounds. Add your words to this list. Write a short poem about each of the shapes, as shown in the example.

Falling
Feathers
Brown
Leaves
Colors
Frost
Pumpkin

_____
_____
_____
_____
_____

Ghosts and goblins,
Witches and bats.
Halloween time
Is scary—like that!

BOO!

Cut out the fall shapes and use them to decorate your home.

SUMMER SIZZLERS

NAME _____

Write briefly about four "fun" things you did this summer. Make a simple "shape" drawing of each on construction paper. Write the appropriate sentence(s) from this page on each of the shapes. Cut out the shapes and hang them on an old wire hanger. Make a sizzler mobile!

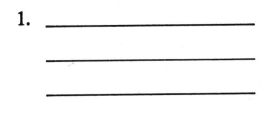

SUMMER SIZZLER

I caught a snake at camp.

I caught two blue gills in the pond.

I found seashells on the beach.

I climbed a huge tree in August

1. _____
_____
_____
_____
_____

2. _____
_____
_____
_____
_____

3. _____
_____
_____
_____
_____

4. _____
_____
_____
_____
_____

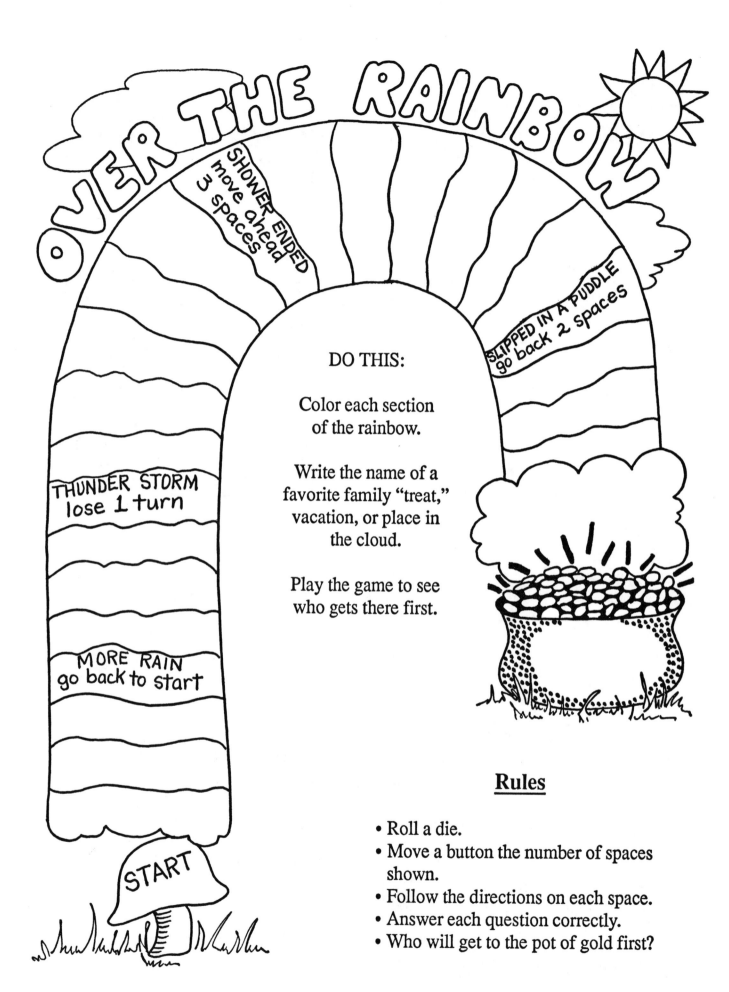

OVER THE RAINBOW

SHOWER ENDED move ahead 3 spaces

SLIPPED IN A PUDDLE go back 2 spaces

DO THIS:

Color each section of the rainbow.

Write the name of a favorite family "treat," vacation, or place in the cloud.

Play the game to see who gets there first.

THUNDER STORM lose 1 turn

MORE RAIN go back to start

START

Rules

- Roll a die.
- Move a button the number of spaces shown.
- Follow the directions on each space.
- Answer each question correctly.
- Who will get to the pot of gold first?

Chapter 2

GO FOR THE GOLD

EAT BREAKFAST EVERYDAY · *TAKE TIME FOR FUN* · *GET ENOUGH SLEEP* · *PRACTICE FIRE DRILLS* · *EAT LESS FAT* · *SMILE* · *EXERCISE REGULARLY* · *EAT HEALTHY SNACKS* · *DO HOME SAFETY CHECKS* · *LAUGH AND PLAY* · *EAT FRUITS AND VEGETABLES*

The title of this Health and Safety chapter says it all: Be the best that you can! We hope this message comes through in the variety of subjects we touch on in this chapter.

Keeping safe and staying healthy are major themes for the primary grades. All of the rules and "messages" in this chapter have been heard before, but we think they are important enough to review again and again.

Today's world provides many choices and opportunities for young people. Some are appealing for the wrong reasons. Some are unattractive due to the nature of the consequences. We have made an effort to focus on some of these problems and provide opportunities for students to think carefully and make responsible decisions. Discussion groups should follow these activities.

As a teacher, your role is to provide a "kaleidoscope" of information on personal health and personal safety. We hope our pages will assist in reinforcing your teachings. You have an important task!

When you feel down, just remember: it takes 43 muscles to frown, but only 17 to smile. Keep smiling!

GO FOR THE GOLD
(Health and Safety)

THE HEALTHY WAY TO GO

What can you and your family do to stay healthy?
Here are some things to think about. Check the things that might help you
become a healthier person. Copy those things on the "people pattern" below.

– Get regular health
  checkups.

– Eat fresh fruits and
  vegetables.

– Exercise.

– Obey safety rules.

– Don't skip meals.

– See dentist.

– Eat less fat.

– Get enough sleep.

– Get eye checkup.

– Eat fewer snacks.

– Talk and plan together.

MORE TO DO: Trace and cut out a "people pattern" for each member of your
family. Discuss good health habits at home. Write health hints on your cutouts.
Tape them to your refrigerator to serve as reminders.

NAME

Get to know these important words. They could save someone's life!

Find these words in the dictionary, then write the meaning of each word in its circle.

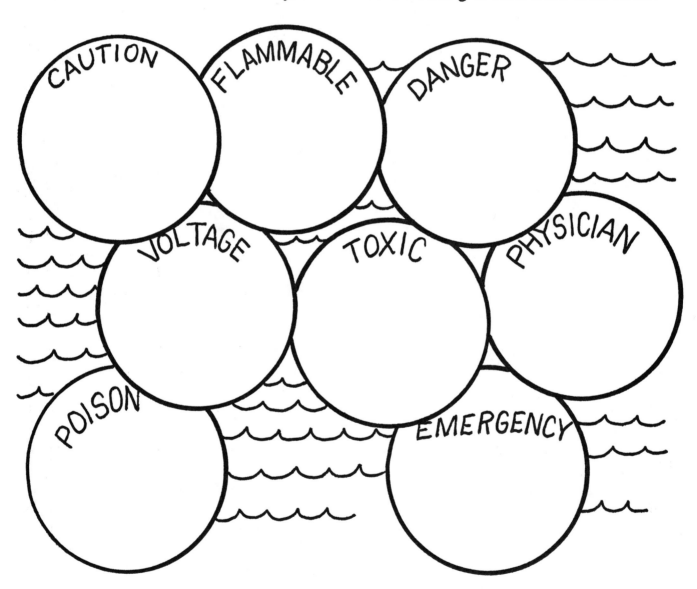

TO DO: Cut the center circle out of a paper plate. Write the words around the edge of the plate. Bring this "life saver" home to share with others.

FIRE SAFETY

CHECKLIST

The sounds of sirens and bells frighten all of us! Do you know that most fires in the home are caused by carelessness? Complete this list, then take it home to talk over with your family.

	Yes	No
1. Chimney is cleaned.		
2. Checked for electric overload.		
3. Combustibles stored carefully.		
4. Areas free of trash and rags.		
5. Kerosene heater in safe place.		
6. Have an escape plan.		
7. Have a fireplace screen.		
8. Have a smoke detector.		
9. Keep matches in a safe place.		
10.		
11.		
12.		

Make an escape plan with a classmate. Share it with your class.

not bragging, but...

Maybe I'm not the greatest.
I can't do it all, you know!
Some things I've not ever tried,
Others I'd not want to show.

We all can do something special,
Better than all the rest.
But the "ME" that doesn't always shine
Is the "ME" that I like the best!

TO DO:
Think about yourself.
Make a list of some things you can do,
and feel proud of.

1. _____

2. _____

3. _____

4. _____

5. _____

6. _____

7. _____

8. _____

9. _____

Draw yourself in this frame.

MORE TO DO: Make a poster
advertising yourself doing your best!

SPORTS Poetry
Spelling
Babysitting
DRAWING MUSIC
WRITING

NAME _____

There are *some* decisions that can be made for us—others we must make our-selves. Which book to choose? Which movie to see? Which college to go to? Which career to pursue? Decisions become more important as we grow older.

STEPS TO A DECISION

1. Write down the choice or decision to be made. _____

_____

2. Make a list of possible solutions. (A) _____

(B) _____ (C) _____

3. Think of and list reasons for each possible solution's being favorable or unfavorable.

	Favorable	Unfavorable
(A)	_____	_____
	_____	_____
	_____	_____
(B)	_____	_____
	_____	_____
	_____	_____
(C)	_____	_____
	_____	_____
	_____	_____

4. Make your decision! _____

_____

5. How do you feel about your choice? _____

_____

HELP! we need AIR

Secondhand smoke is bad for our health. When we breathe in the smoke from cigarettes, cigars, and pipes that others are smoking, it pollutes our lungs. Is that fair?

TO DO: Read the following and write down what **YOU** would do.

You and your family are celebrating your birthday by going to your favorite restaurant. Although your Mom asked for a non-smoking section, the hostess seats you at a table next to a man smoking a cigar. What would you do?

_____

_____

_____

You share a bedroom with your older brother. One evening you are reading in bed when he comes in smoking a cigarette. What would you do?

_____

_____

You and your friend are waiting for her parents to pick you up after a basketball game. When the car arrives, you see that both adults in the car are smoking. What can you do?

_____

MORE TO DO: Make a NO SMOKING poster to hang on the door of your room.

CLEAN AIR IS EVERYONE'S RIGHT

PLUGGER

The Happy Fire Hydrant

Use this space to write a story about "Plugger"
and how he helps us.

_____

_____

_____

_____

_____

_____

_____

_____

notes on a COUCH POTATO

Exercise is important for both the mind and the body!

DO THIS: Keep an accurate log of time spent on both strenuous and non-strenuous activity for five days.

I GET LOTS OF EXERCISE, MOM. I'VE MADE 3 TRIPS TO THE KITCHEN DURING THE LAST MOVIE.

	MONDAY	TUESDAY	WEDNESDAY	THURSDAY	FRIDAY
Exercise					
TV, Sitting Around, Etc.					

How did you do? _____

Now what? _____

_____

Name _____

Your teacher has put some skills on this gameboard. Play the game when you are feeling better.

GET WELL SOON. WE MISS YOU.

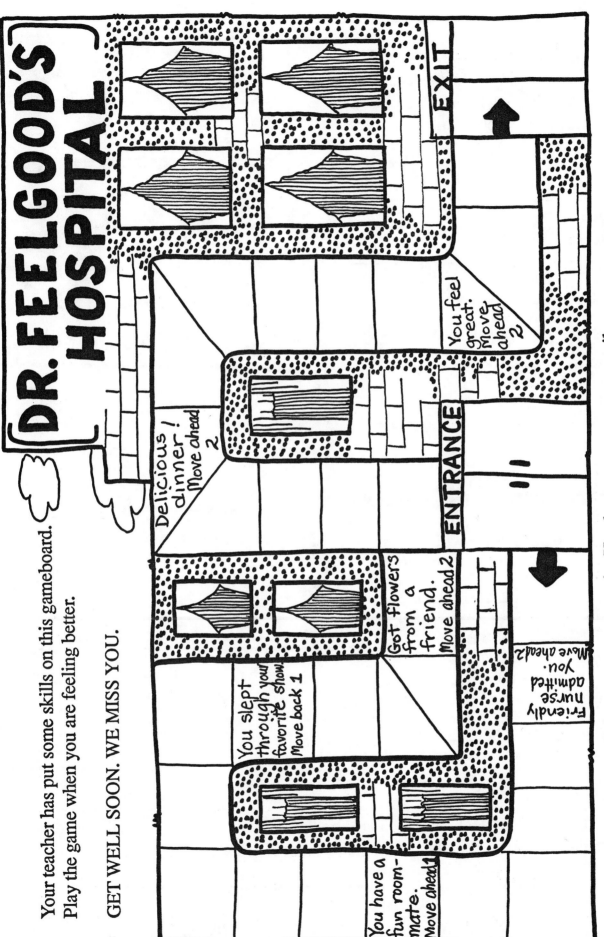

DR. FEELGOOD'S HOSPITAL

EXIT

ENTRANCE

Delicious dinner! Move ahead 2

You feel great. Move ahead 2

You slept through your favorite show. Move back 1

Got flowers from a friend. Move ahead 2

Friendly nurse admitted you. Move ahead 2

You have a fun room-mate. Move ahead 1

Take turns—toss a coin. Heads move two spaces—tails move one space.
Complete the skill and follow the arrows. Get well soon!

Sometimes it's hard to verbalize thinking. Try to show how you feel on each continuum. This provides a good way for us to learn more about ourselves.

EXAMPLE

I am on time.

Never   Louis   Eileen   Always

What do you think? Put your "X" on each continuum below.

What do you think? Put your "X" on each continuum below.

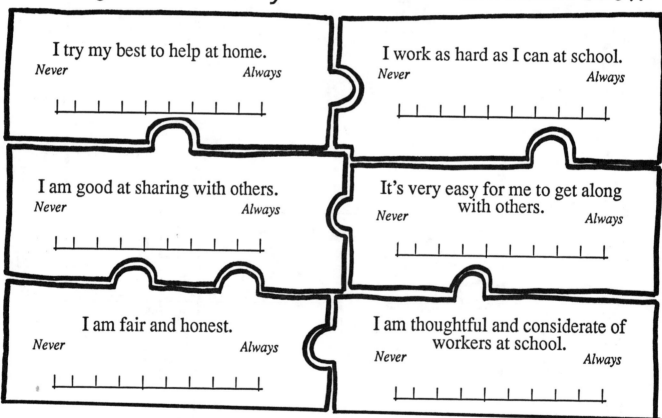

I try my best to help at home.
Never   Always

I work as hard as I can at school.
Never   Always

I am good at sharing with others.
Never   Always

It's very easy for me to get along with others.
Never   Always

I am fair and honest.
Never   Always

I am thoughtful and considerate of workers at school.
Never   Always

MORE TO DO: Make four continuums on the back of this page. Give the page to a friend or someone at home to complete. Talk about it together.

WHAT'S IMPORTANT ??????????????

Friends will come and go; some may last a lifetime! What qualities do you think make good friends?

TO DO: Read each descriptor, then decide how important these things are to you. Make a check mark to show how you feel.

These Things Are:	Very Important	Important	Not Important
1. Good looking			
2. Lots of money			
3. Super family			
4. Smart			
5. Funny			
6. Fancy house			
7. Shares things			
8. Popular			
9. Good manners			
10. Sensitive			
11. Loyal			
12. Caring			
13. Considerate			
14. Generous			
15. Dependable			
16. Trustworthy			
17. Honest			

MORE TO DO: Now go over this list with a friend or classmate. Do you have different opinions? Write about this on the back of this page.

Assessing Friendship
©1992 by Incentive Publications, Inc., Nashville, TN

○ ○ ○ ○ ○ ○ PULSE PARTNERS ○ ○ ○ ○ ○

Do you know that when we exercise we help our heart and lungs to become more efficient? If you exercise and are physically fit, you can take part in sports and games without getting tired.

DO THIS:

1. Measure your pulse rate. Place your index and middle fingers on the inside of your wrist. Practice this until you can do it easily.
2. Take a classmate's pulse. Count the beats you hear in ten seconds.
3. Multiply that number by six to get your rate for one minute.
4. Write that number on the chart.
5. Have your partner jog in place for one minute, then record another pulse rate.
6. Reverse. Now your partner will take your pulse and record it.

	Heartbeats Before Exercise	Heartbeats After Exercise
You		
Partner		

JUST FOR FUN! Draw a line from the number of heartbeats to the picture you think it represents. Don't peek at the answers.

HEARTBEATS

35

70-80

600

120

sometimes I get ANGRY

Every morning you and Pat walk to school together. One day when you stop at Pat's house, his Mom tells you that he left early to walk with someone else.

Enough to make you mad?
What might you do?

_____

_____

_____

Your sister wore your favorite sweater to school one day without asking you. She got a spot on the front of it. You caught her putting it back in the drawer.

You were furious!
What would you do?

_____

_____

_____

What are some things you can do when you are angry?

Talk with someone about your feelings. Don't pretend that nothing hurts.

Clear the air and tell your friend. Discussion usually helps you feel better.

You fill in.

On the back of this sheet make a list of things that can hurt, or that can make you angry. Compare this list with a friend. Talk about how to manage the anger.

REMEMBER—it's okay to get angry!

AGREE-DISAGREE

A difference of opinion is okay! When we disagree with a friend, it is important to allow the other person's opinion.

Mark the boxes below.

	Agree	Disagree
1. Chocolate is the best ice cream.	☐	☐
2. Dogs make better pets than cats.	☐	☐
3. Kids should work for their allowances.	☐	☐
4. Baseball is better than football.	☐	☐
5. More people like hotdogs than hamburgers.	☐	☐

TO DO: Color the "A" and "D" at the top of the page. Cut out each letter and paste it on cardboard. As your teacher reads a list of questions, hold up the "A" to agree and the "D" when you disagree.

HELP--IT'S AN EMERGENCY

911

DOCTOR_____

POLICE _____

NEIGHBOR_____

To report a fire or medical emergency in many towns, you can dial "911."
Do you know how to dial from where you live? _____

DO THIS: Write important numbers on the telephone above. Cut it out and tape
it to your refrigerator at home. BE READY FOR AN EMERGENCY!

What would you say if there was a fire? _____

_____

If someone needed medical help? _____

_____

How would you tell how to get to your home? _____

_____

_____

NO! NOT ME

Sometimes kids are encouraged by their peers to try things they know are not good for them. Write your response to what a "friend" is saying in the talking balloon.

Have a drag. A little smoke won't hurt.

YOU

Here, take a sip. It's only cheap wine.

YOU

Why not try this chewing tobacco? All the "pros" use it.

YOU

Select one of these topics and make a "SAY NO" poster on the back of this sheet.

WHICH CAR IS MAKING A HAPPY TRIP?

Traveling with family or friends can be fun. Remember these safety rules.

_____ Always wear seat belts, even when going a short distance.

_____ Never distract the driver.

_____ Don't stick your head or hands out the window.

_____ Never throw things out the window.

DO THIS: Use this space to help make a page for a HAPPY TRIP BOOK. You may want to make up a game to include: cars, colors, animals, letters on signs, license plates, shapes, mile markers, maps; or write a short story, puzzle, or poems. Your teacher will make copies for you and your classmates to have on your next HAPPY TRIP!

HAPPY TRIP

DO I KNOW YOU?

Be Safe: Don't Go With Strangers!

Read the sentences below. Read the word list. Write one word from the list in each blank.

1. _____ go with a stranger.

2. Check with an _____ before you ride with someone.

3. Stay with the _____ in the grocery store.

4. It isn't smart to take _____ from strangers.

5. Never _____ away when in a store with an adult.

6. Always _____ the sitter where you are going.

7. Most people can be _____.

8. Be safe, don't take _____.

WORD LIST
candy
tell
trusted
adult
never
cart
chances
wander

Have you ever had a problem with a stranger?

Share what happened with your class.

We all know that some foods are better for us than are others. Junk foods may taste good, but should not be eaten too often.

Fit the names of these junk foods into the puzzle.

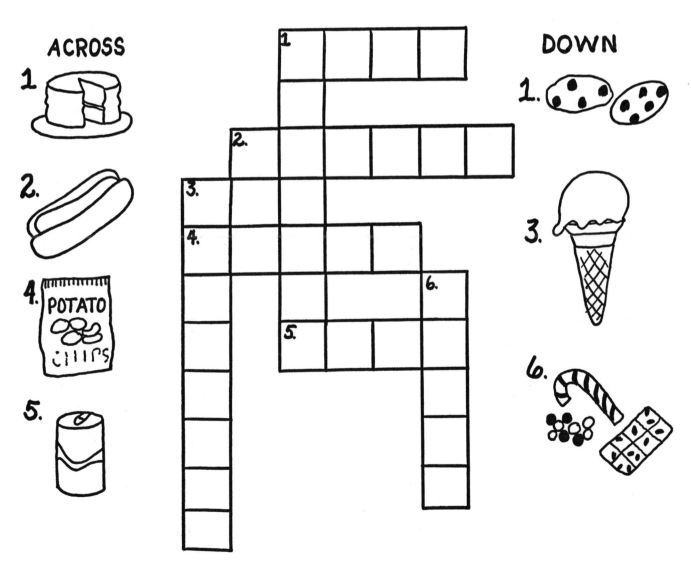

ACROSS

1.
2.
4. POTATO CHIPS
5.

DOWN

1.
3.
6.

Reviewing Junk Food Words
©1992 by Incentive Publications, Inc., Nashville, TN

NAME _____

are you ever LONELY?

"You Bet I Am!

Don't like the food they give me; won't let my buddies come in the yard; make me walk when I'm dog-tired; fleas are bad . . .

What's *your* problem?"

Some things that make us lonely: What about . . .

1. Losing a friend _____

2. Being left out _____

3. Not enough friends _____

4. Parents never home _____

5. Adult "nagging" _____

6. No brothers or sisters _____

7. (other) _____

_____

What are some things we can do about loneliness?

_____

_____

_____

_____

cheer up

A get-well card is a good way to share your feelings. Help make someone feel better. Make up a verse for this card. Then add some pictures. Give it to someone who is not well.

Cheer Up!

Get well soon!
Don't be sick.
I miss your tune,
Come back quick.
(Like a flash!)

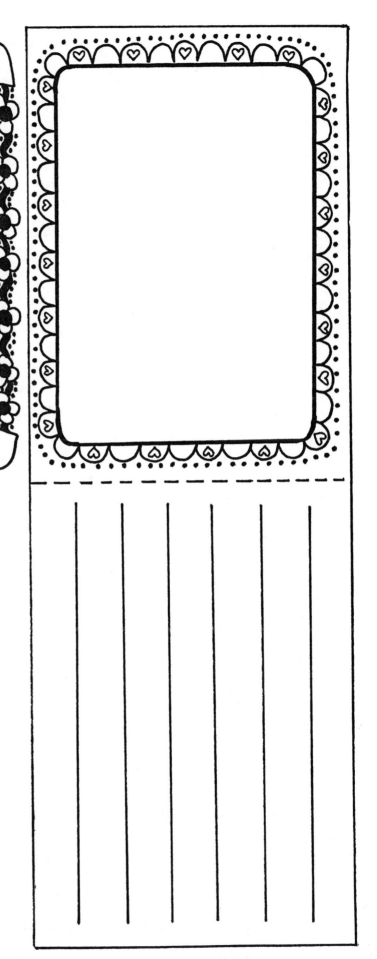

your PEER group

> PEERS are people near your own age. They are your equals in many ways.

> PEERS include friends and classmates, girls and boys.

> PEERS have fun and learn from one another. They often form groups.

> PEERS grow older. You will have many circles of peers as you go through life.

PEER PRESSURE (when people try to make you do or act or look a certain way) can be a problem. What can you do when faced with peer pressure?

DO THIS: Write your ideas after each suggestion. Share these with your group or class.

1. Communicate! _____

_____

2. Be Yourself! _____

_____

3. Respect feelings of friends and family. _____

_____

4. Find other friends. _____

_____

REMEMBER: It's not always easy to stand up to your peers!

IS THIS HOUSE SICK!

NAME _____

Did you know that houses can make you sick?
Here are some sources of indoor pollution.
Check off the things you know about.
Learn more about the others.

___ Radon gas

___ Pesticide storage

___ Fumes from paints and
varnishes

___ Fumes from unvented gas
stoves and dryers

___ Fibers from asbestos tiles and
insulation

___ Vapors from dry cleaning

___ Bacteria-filled humidifiers

___ Gases from aerosol cans

___ Lead dust from old paint

___ Smoke from wood stoves

___ Car exhaust in garage

___ Vapors from cleaning products

___ Lead and chemicals in
drinking water

FOLLOW-UP: Take this list home for a house checkup. How did your house do?

_____

_____

_____

Family Ties

Families come in different sizes, shapes, colors, numbers, and sexes. Some are all mixed up and that's okay.

TO DO: Write the name of each member of your family. Draw a family picture. Share this with your teacher or a friend.

_____
_____
_____
_____
_____
_____
_____
_____

YOUR FAMILY

Chapter 3
PANNING FOR GOLD WITH LANGUAGE ARTS

The knowledge of and enjoyment of words are the keys to a good language arts curriculum. In this chapter we provide opportunities for primary students to begin reading their own words. Familiarity with language and pride of "authorship" form the essence of successful language experience.

The rhythm, cadence, and music-like quality of simple rhymes catch the imagination of young people. For this reason we've included a number of our own poems and we encourage the writing of others.

The reading of poetry can be tedious, so we suggest it be presented as a "listening" activity. The thoughts, "melody," and sensory images can be appreciated more when read aloud by the teacher.

Reading, thinking, and writing skills are dominant in these pages. We use a four-step process: (1) The pupil is provided with an idea, or written facts and information. (2) The pupil is asked to think about the topic and develop ideas. (3) The pupil is asked to write about the topic and his or her ideas. (4) Time to share is provided. (It's important to share the completed work and listen to the ideas of others.)

Imagination and creativity play a big part in our workpages. A sense of humor and our light-hearted topics will keep the activities appealing and fun to do.

Daily vocabulary development is essential; we suggest bombarding young people with words. Begin this practice in kindergarten, where clearly-written labels can identify almost everything in the classroom. In the middle grades, written word lists will help in the writing process. This visible "word presence" will provide a sense of comfort and make it possible to use new words in assignments. Personal dictionaries or vocabulary lists can provide positive growth for all students.

With all that the contemporary curriculum demands and offers, it can be difficult to find the time for all that you plan. Language skills, however, can be integrated into almost everything you do during the school day.

Ideally, growth through "sharing" and reading will continue when children go home at the end of the school day. Turn your students on to words. It will "pay off" for a lifetime!

PANNING FOR GOLD
(Language Arts)

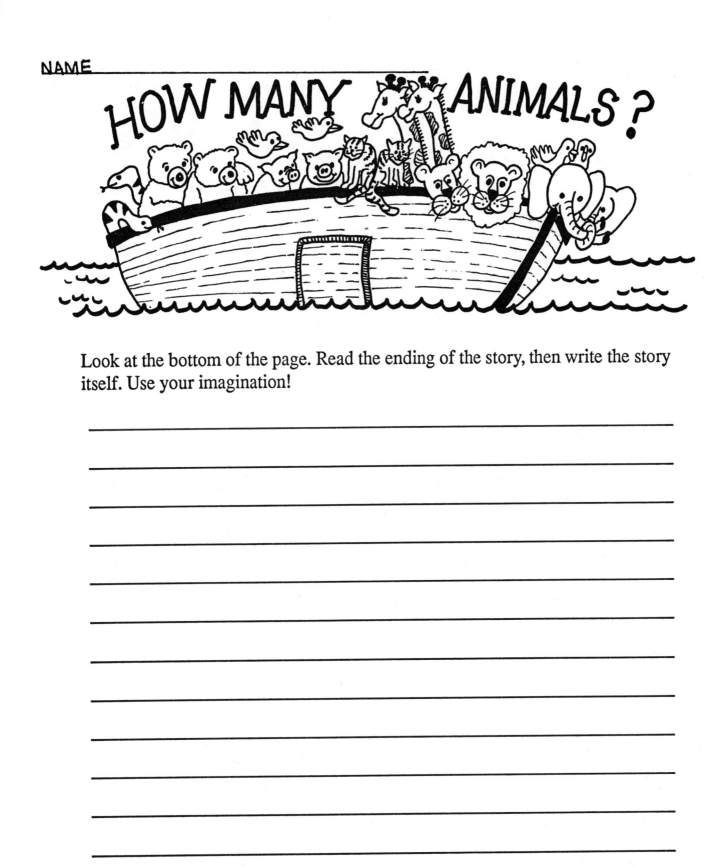

HOW MANY ANIMALS?

Look at the bottom of the page. Read the ending of the story, then write the story itself. Use your imagination!

_____

_____

_____

_____

_____

_____

_____

_____

_____

_____

_____

_____

As the boat went out to sea, we could hear the happy sounds of farewell and the lions roaring—"Row, Row, Row . . ."

A TIME FOR HEROES

Heroes help us to find good in ourselves. They give us inspiration. When we look up to someone, we work harder to achieve what we want to be.

Kirk wants to be a body builder like Arnold Schwarzenegger.

Martin Luther King is a hero to Jessie.

Mark wants to play football like Joe Montana.

Kim. wants to sing with a group. She likes Whitney Houston.

Who is your hero? Who do you look up to? Write a letter to that special person telling why he or she is important to you.

Dear _____:

_____

_____

_____

_____

_____

_____

_____

_____

Sincerely,

your picture...

READING YOUR OWN WORDS IS FUN!

Choose one of the three activities listed below and draw a circle around your choice. Then draw a picture of the activity in the picture frame below.

1. Yourself playing in the park.
2. Yourself on a picnic with your friends.
3. Yourself on a vacation with your family.

Write a sentence telling about your picture.

_____

_____

Read the sentence to your teacher.
Read the sentence to a friend.
Take this page home. Show the picture and read the sentence.

DO YOU KNOW WHAT IT TAKES TO BECOME A PRINCIPAL OR CUSTODIAN, A NURSE OR MUSIC TEACHER?

HELP WANTED

TO DO:

Find out about someone who works in your school. Ask questions of that person to help you learn about that person's job. Find out what he or she does, how he or she does it, and what kind of training he or she needed to get the job. Use the back of this page for your notes. Using the information you learned, write a newspaper "Help Wanted" advertisement in the space below. You may want to check your newspaper for wording and format ideas.

●●●●●● CLASSIFIED ●●●●●●●

WE NEED YOU!

_____ _____

_____ _____

_____ _____

_____ _____

_____ _____

_____ _____

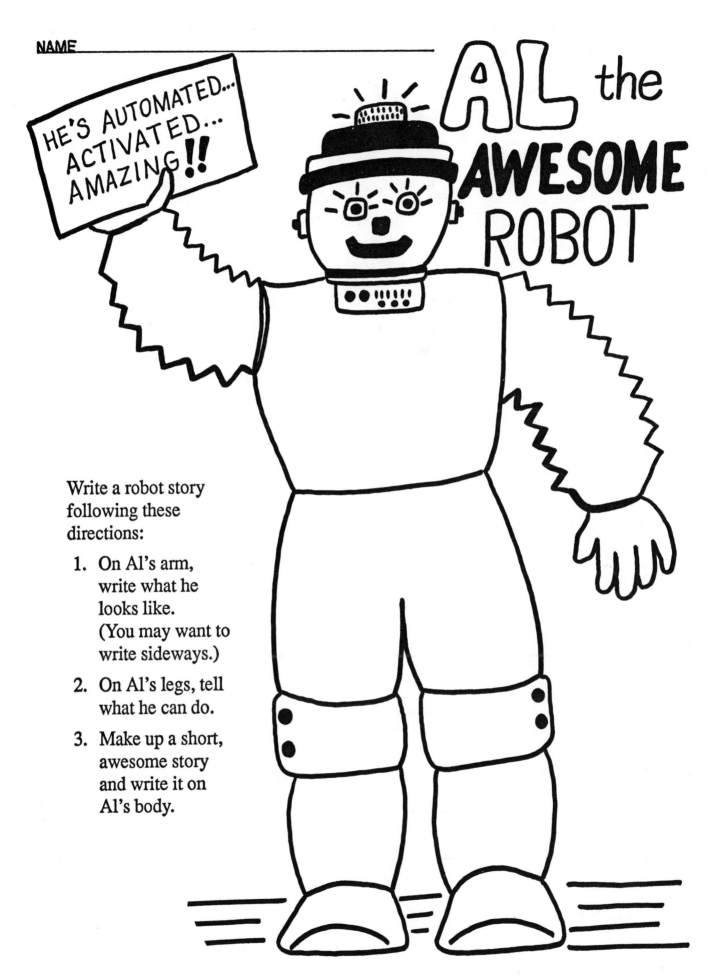

AL the **AWESOME ROBOT**

HE'S AUTOMATED... ACTIVATED... AMAZING!!

Write a robot story following these directions:

1. On Al's arm, write what he looks like. (You may want to write sideways.)

2. On Al's legs, tell what he can do.

3. Make up a short, awesome story and write it on Al's body.

WHO'S A DREAMER?

HEAD IN THE CLOUDS

*Read the story carefully, then answer the
questions below.*

Megan was a whiz in English class, but she had
trouble understanding math. The other kids often laughed at
her when she could not answer a simple math question. She
would blush and squirm in her seat, then put her head down
in embarrassment. "Megan, aren't you paying
attention?" the teacher would demand.

Megan *was* a daydreamer. She walked around
deep in thought most of the time. She thought about books and people and made
up stories in her head. She loved writing stories for her English teacher.

One day the English teacher handed back some papers to the class. She had a
frown on her face. "I'm surprised at you, class," she said. "Not only have you
forgotten how to spell, most of you didn't have much to write about. I'd like you
to do these over and hand in some real stories."

Megan was surprised at the groans from her classmates. "I don't know what to
write!" they complained. Megan offered to help.

By gently asking questions, Megan inspired her friends to think of some good
ideas for stories. She helped them with their spelling, too! They grew ashamed of
the way they had teased her in math class.

Now when Megan can't work math problems, her classmates try to help. She
still has her head in the clouds—but she's also learning important basic math!

1. Megan was not a good_____student.

2. How did her classmates treat her? _____

3. Was her teacher understanding? _____

4. Do you think Megan was dumb?_____

5. What happened to make Megan's classmates feel differently about her?_____

_____

6. Do you know someone like Megan? _____

7. How could you help this person?_____

_____

NAME

report

Good reporting usually includes these five "W" ingredients. Choose a picture from a newspaper or magazine. Think about it, then make up a story. Write your report below.

Who _____

_____

_____

What _____

_____

_____

Why _____

_____

_____

When _____

_____

Where _____

_____

_____

Don't forget to attach your picture to the story.

A STORY SANDWICH

It Has A Beginning, An Ending, And Lots Of Filling!

Use this space to write a delicious story. Be sure to add a "garnish" of pickles and seasonings to spice it up!

BEGINNING

MIDDLE

ENDING

YEAR OF THE BOOK

This year try something different

BOOK MOBILE

Cut out six shapes that say something about the book. Write a paragraph about the book on each shape. Color your pictures, and tie them to a wire hanger with string.

Date Completed

BOOK JACKET

Fold your paper to make a book cover. Draw an illustration on the front and write a synopsis on the sections that are folded inside (flyleaves). Write about the author on the back of the cover. (You may need to do some research on the author.)

Date Completed

BOOK BOX

Cover the sides of a shoebox. In the box, place several items (or pictures of things) from the story. Write a paragraph on a note card about each item. Decorate the sides of the box according to the theme.

SILHOUETTE

Make a large drawing of the head of one character from your book. (Use your imagination.) Tell about that character on the back. Explain why you liked, or did not like this person.

Date Completed

POSTCARDS

Cut out four postcard-sized pieces of posterboard. Make a drawing of something from the book on the front of each. Write a message on the back of each. Be sure to include "happenings" from the story.

Date Completed

BOOK REPORTS can be fun!

NAME _____

FRUIT BOWL HANGUPS

PEACHY A POEM

Sweet and juicy,
What a treat!
A favorite fruit
I love to eat.

On cereal
Or in a pie.
A peach is best—
Oh me, oh my!

TOP BANANA

Think about your favorite fruits. Write some "fruity" words around the edge of this sheet.

Use the words to make up a poem for each shape.

Make more shapes for other fruit poems. Hang them around your classroom or at home.

WONDERFUL WATERMELON

＿＿ENDERS

How Creative Can You Be?
Read these sentences carefully, then write a creative ending for each.

1. It rained so hard that _____

   _____

2. When my Aunt sneezed _____

   _____

3. Suddenly the pepperoni pizza _____

   _____

4. We got in the canoe and_____

   _____

5. The alligator was _____

   _____

6. Look, the dolphin_____

   _____

7. Out of the trash can came _____

   _____

8. The ride on the ferris wheel _____

   _____

Now that you have been creative, choose
one sentence to turn into a paragraph. Use
the back of this page.

Put your pencil to work.

It's important to follow directions.

Follow these directions. Check off each number after you perform each activity.

☐ 1. Draw a boat in the water.

☐ 2. Make three windows on the boat.

☐ 3. Draw a face in the middle window.

☐ 4. Draw a bird to the right of the cloud.

☐ 5. Make rays around the sun.

☐ 6. Put a palm tree on the island.

☐ 7. Draw a small sailboat behind the island.

☐ 8. Put birds wherever you want them.

☐ 9. Give your picture a title.

☐ 10. Color your picture.

THE LETTER BARREL

↓ start

c _ r   p _ e   _ _ _ _   gi _ l   hors _   _ _ _ _ _

mou _ e

You can play this game alone or with a friend. The words on the gameboard have missing letters and picture clues.

1. Look in the barrel for the missing letters.
2. Cover each letter you use with an "X."
3. Add the letter to the word.
4. You may use each letter only once.

ri _ g

ca _ e

m _ on

h	o	k	r	e
u	i	a	e	n
n	s	d	u	u
s	e	e	c	o
k	t	o	k	t
i	e	p	f	i
t	i	x	k	s

nes _

goa _

b _ ke

soc _

NOW.
What letter is left in the barrel? _

lea _

_ _ _ _   K _ y   ap _ le   b _ ar   f _ sh   bo _ t

high tech wizard

This is a most technologically advanced computer system. What can it do? It will help you develop a bigger vocabulary!

DO THIS: Make a collection of old bottle caps. Cut out small paper circles to fit inside the caps. On each circle, write a new vocabulary word to study. Write each word twice. Turn the words over and mix them up. Play "concentration" with a friend.

TO PLAY: Say each word you turn over. When you find a "match," put the two identical words in your pile. The winner is the person who has the most words at the end of the game.

CHICKEN OR THE EGG?

It's usually easy to tell what happens first.
Put a "1" under the picture that shows what happened first. Put a "2" under the picture that shows what happened next. Then tell why you ordered each one as you did.

Because _____

_____

_____

_____

Because _____

_____

_____

_____

Because _____

_____

_____

_____

Because _____

_____

_____

_____

Share This With Others

SOME THING FISHY

Make a Fishing Game
to help you study your
spelling words.

TO DO:

1. Trace these shapes, making one for each of your spelling words.
2. Write each spelling word on a shape.
3. Put a paper clip on each shape.
4. Make a fishing pole with string, a pencil, and a magnet.
5. Take turns going fishing with a friend. Catch a word and have your partner read it to you.
6. Spell the word.

GOOD LUCK!

THE REST OF THE STORY

After all these years, haven't you wondered what happened to good old "Jack And Jill?"

Here's the rest of the story.

Jack and Jill went up the hill
To fetch a pail of water.

Jack fell down and broke his crown
And Jill came tumbling after.

A kindly man (his name was Sam)
Took them to the doctor.

The doctor said,"No, you're not dead—
You'll be fine tomorrow."

DO THIS: Pick one of your favorite childhood nursery rhymes. Write it in the space below. Make up an ending—tell us "the rest of the story."

SMACKER JACKS

When you opened your box of "Smacker Jacks," you found the most incredible prize. Write a story about what happened. Use your imagination!

SMACKER JACKS

YOU'LL SMACK YOUR LIPS WHEN YOU EAT THIS DELICIOUS POPCORN.

★ ★ ★ A PRIZE IN EVERY PACKAGE

**Do You Know That
Each Year An Award Is Given For
The Most Imaginative "Tall Story?"**

TO DO: Do you know the story of Paul Bun-
yan? That's a tall tale! Write *your* tall tale.

_____

_____

_____

_____

_____

_____

_____

_____

_____

_____

_____

_____

_____

_____

_____

_____

_____

_____

AN OUTRAGEOUSLY TALL TALE

COMING CLOSER AND CLOSER TO US, WAS WHAT APPEARED TO BE...

NAME_____

Pure Gold Can Be Found Right In Your Own Library.
Let's Find Out More About It!

TO DO: Take this sheet with you to your library. Fill in the blanks. Don't be afraid to ask for help and direction!

1. The librarian's name is_____ .

2. Books may be kept out for _____ . Fines are _____ .

3. The catalog code numbers in the History section are _____ .

4. The catalog code numbers in the Science section are _____ .

5. The catalog code numbers in the Art section are_____ .

6. How can you find a biography?_____ .

7. How many titles are written by the author Judy Blum? _____

8. Can you find Moby Dick in your library? _____

9. Who is the author of Moby Dick? _____

10. What is the name of a magazine that looks interesting? _____

11. What is the title of your favorite book?_____

12. Look for that book. What book is next to it on the shelf? _____

13. How many sets of encyclopedias are there? _____

14. The encyclopedias are in the _____ section .

15. Look for a map of your state. What is the name of the book in which you found it?_____

16. Check out one book while you are in the library. What is the title and who is the author? _____

Digging For "Gold" In Your Library Can Be Fun!

Name _____

Name _____

Name _____

Name _____

POETRY THAT MAKES SENSE
FROM ANY ANGLE!

A Triangular Triplet is a short poem of three lines. All lines rhyme, and they can be read in any order.

> Try this as a team of four.

Working together, make up four triplets. When you have finished, write them around the edge of a construction paper kite. Hang the kite in your classroom.

A. _____

_____

_____

_____

B. _____

_____

_____

_____

C. _____

_____

_____

_____

Flying Triplets

Kites fly high
up in the sky.
I know why

Flowers of pink
I'll give it a drink.
It's dry I think

D. _____

_____

_____

_____

haiku FOR YOU

Not a poet, you say? Don't like to rhyme? Then learn to write this very simple form of poetry. Haiku originated in Japan hundreds of years ago.

Writing and reading Haiku is still a popular way to celebrate the seasons.

HAIKU PATTERN
Line 1 = Five syllables
Line 2 = Seven syllables
Line 3 = Five syllables

DO THIS: Cut out a picture showing your favorite season. Paste it in the box. Study the picture and think about why you like that season. Write a few words that describe that time of year.

SEASONAL WORDS

_____

_____

_____

Use the space below for your Haiku.

_____

_____

_____

_____

WINTER
Snowflakes falling down.
I catch them on my lashes.
Delicious winter.

Paste seasonal picture ⬇⬇

NAME _____

XYZ CEREAL

You'll Find Lots Of Good Reading On A Cereal Box!

TO DO: Cut the bottom from an empty cereal box. Cut open one side and spread the box out flat. Read your cereal box carefully and answer the following questions.

1. Name of cereal _____

2. Weight of package _____ How many grams of fat? _____

3. Name and address of company _____

   _____

4. What is the first ingredient? _____

5. How much iron is in the cereal? _____

6. Is there a coupon to send for something? _____ What? _____

7. What is advertised on the back? _____

8. Did you learn anything from reading this box? If so, what? _____

   _____

   _____

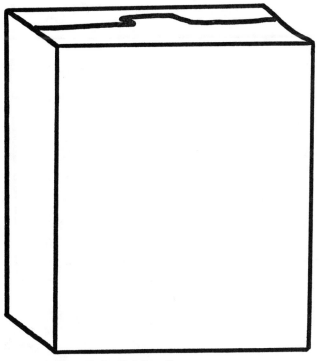

design your own cereal box

- GIVE IT A NAME.
- TELL HOW GOOD IT IS.
- BE SURE TO SAY HOW HEALTHY IT IS!

COULD BE WORSE!

It was the most terrible day you remember! Tell your story.
(It can be real or make-believe.)

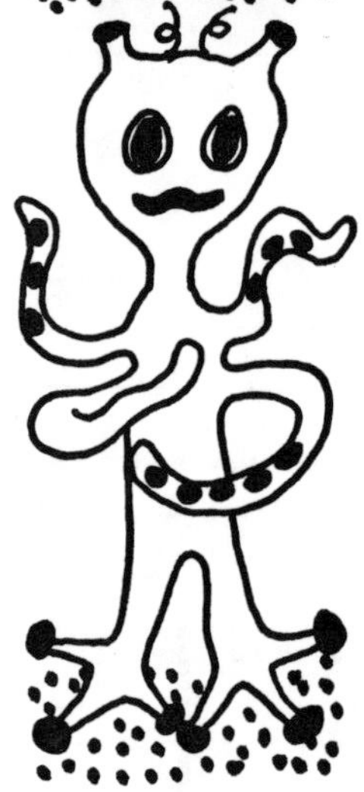

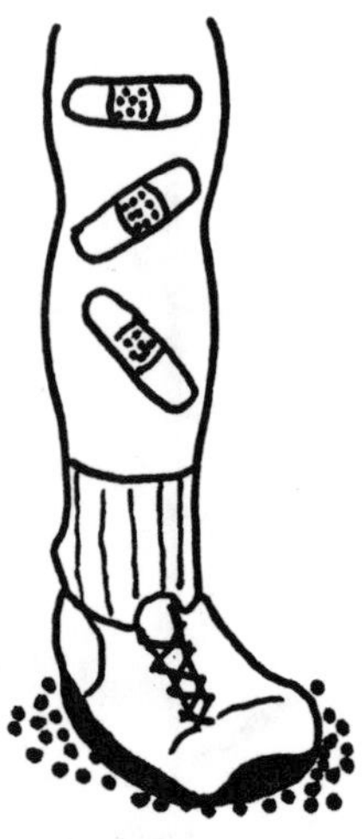

_____

_____

_____

_____

_____

_____

_____

_____

_____

_____

_____

_____

_____

_____

_____

Take heart! Things have a way of getting better! Share this with a friend.

Each New Word Can Be An Adventure In Language!

—Cut this sheet on the broken line.

—Color the cover and add your name.

—Fold thirteen pieces of paper in half like a book.

—Staple this page to the front to make the cover.

—Number each page.

—Make a heading for each page, using every letter of the alphabet.
(Some letters may not need a whole page. Use half pages if you used less paper.)

—Carry this book with you during the school day.

—Whenever you hear an interesting new word, write it in your book.

—Look up the meaning of the new word, or ask for help.

—Write the meaning of the new word in your personal dictionary.

—Have a great adventure in language!

my personal DICTIONARY

YOUR NAME

Buddy 1. _____   Buddy 2. _____

Working as story-writing buddies, select a topic from the list on this page. Take turns writing each part of the story on one buddy's page. When you have finished, go over it together and make corrections or changes. Rewrite your final copy on the other buddy's page.

Title

_____

Beginning   Circle Topic

                                                              Fishing
                                                              Camping
                                                              Biking
                                                              Parades
Middle   Circus
                                                              Friends
                                                              Skateboards
                                                              Goats
                                                              Picnics
                                                              Tree House
More Middle   Mud Puddles
                                                              Rainbows
                                                              Robots
                                                              Spiders
                                                              Attics
                                                              Grandparents
Ending   July
                                                              Airplanes
                                                              Paint
                                                              Gifts
                                                              Dragons
                                                              Parrots
Use the back of this page if you need more space.   Railroads

Chapter 4
STAKE YOUR CLAIM IN THE ENVIRONMENT

Before we can hope that today's young people will improve the world in which we live, they must first learn to appreciate it. The activities in this chapter were designed to encourage students to deepen their awareness of the world around them by using all of their senses.

We urge you to acknowledge the beauty of the environment and the joy that it brings while teaching in your classroom. Show the interdependence of all the animal species, and the necessity for an ecosystem that will support them and provide for their needs.

Help children to become aware of what has happened to their environment because of the growth of cities, pollution of the rivers and streams, depletion of forests and woodlands, toxic dumping and "excesses" in all areas. It's a fact: if every National Park visitor dropped one sheet of paper, the litter could circle our country several times.

Some of the following pages may provide new information for your students; most, however, will reinforce your own teaching. We ask them to think, then explain how they feel. We want them to observe, and to tell what they see. "Recycling" significant information can only reinforce its importance!

As a teacher, your role is very important. Encourage social awareness and feelings of responsibility that will enable young people to make sound choices followed by action. Today's youngsters must develop a sense of pride in what can be theirs—and they must be determined to protect and improve the world in which they live. They can't afford to compromise their future!

STAKE YOUR CLAIM IN THE ENVIRONMENT
(Science and Nature)

FOR A BETTER ENVIRONMENT

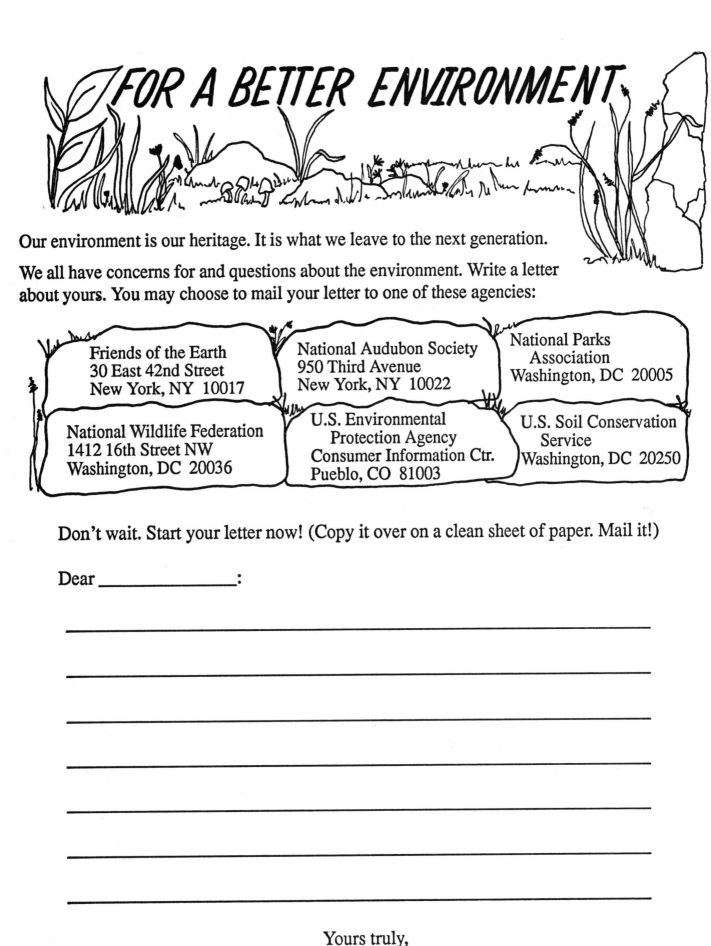

Our environment is our heritage. It is what we leave to the next generation.

We all have concerns for and questions about the environment. Write a letter about yours. You may choose to mail your letter to one of these agencies:

Friends of the Earth
30 East 42nd Street
New York, NY 10017

National Audubon Society
950 Third Avenue
New York, NY 10022

National Parks
Association
Washington, DC 20005

National Wildlife Federation
1412 16th Street NW
Washington, DC 20036

U.S. Environmental
Protection Agency
Consumer Information Ctr.
Pueblo, CO 81003

U.S. Soil Conservation
Service
Washington, DC 20250

Don't wait. Start your letter now! (Copy it over on a clean sheet of paper. Mail it!)

Dear _____:

_____

_____

_____

_____

_____

_____

Yours truly,

_____

PROTECT THE ENVIRONMENT

We must stand up to those who destroy the environment.

The following are important environmental slogans:

* Save the **seals**

* The crocodile is an endangered **species**

* Help save the rain **forest**

* Clean up **toxic** waste dumping

* Our **lungs** are not a landfill

* Preserve the maritime **ecosystem**

* Help the threatened **dolphin**

* **Stop ocean** dumping

* Save the **planet**

TO DO: Circle each **bold** word in the word maze.

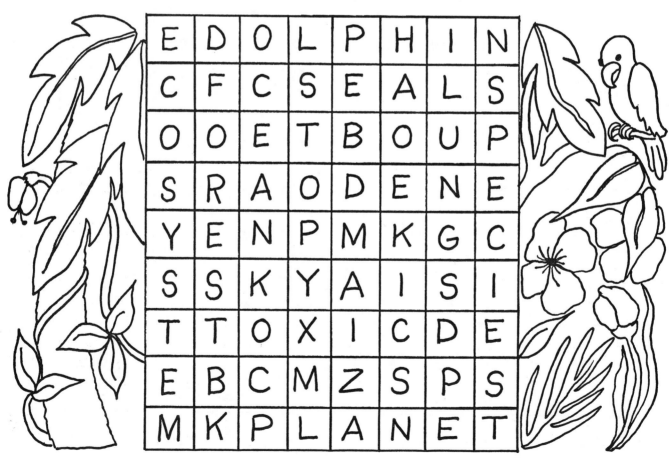

E	D	O	L	P	H	I	N
C	F	C	S	E	A	L	S
O	O	E	T	B	O	U	P
S	R	A	O	D	E	N	E
Y	E	N	P	M	K	G	C
S	S	K	Y	A	I	S	I
T	T	O	X	I	C	D	E
E	B	C	M	Z	S	P	S
M	K	P	L	A	N	E	T

MORE TO DO: Make up a new slogan. Hang it in your classroom.

...AND WHERE DO YOU LIVE?

Our planet is the home for many different kinds of animals.

TO DO:
1. Look at the picture of each animal.
2. Fill in the missing letters.
3. Write the name of the kind of house each animal lives in.
4. If you need help, check the words on the "house" at the bottom of the page.

S P I D _ R

F R _ G

_ ONEYBEE

T U R T L _

C _ A M

W O _ M

L I O _

ROVER

earth   nest
web   shell
pond   sea
den   tree
hive   cave

Why do you think these animal homes are all different? _____

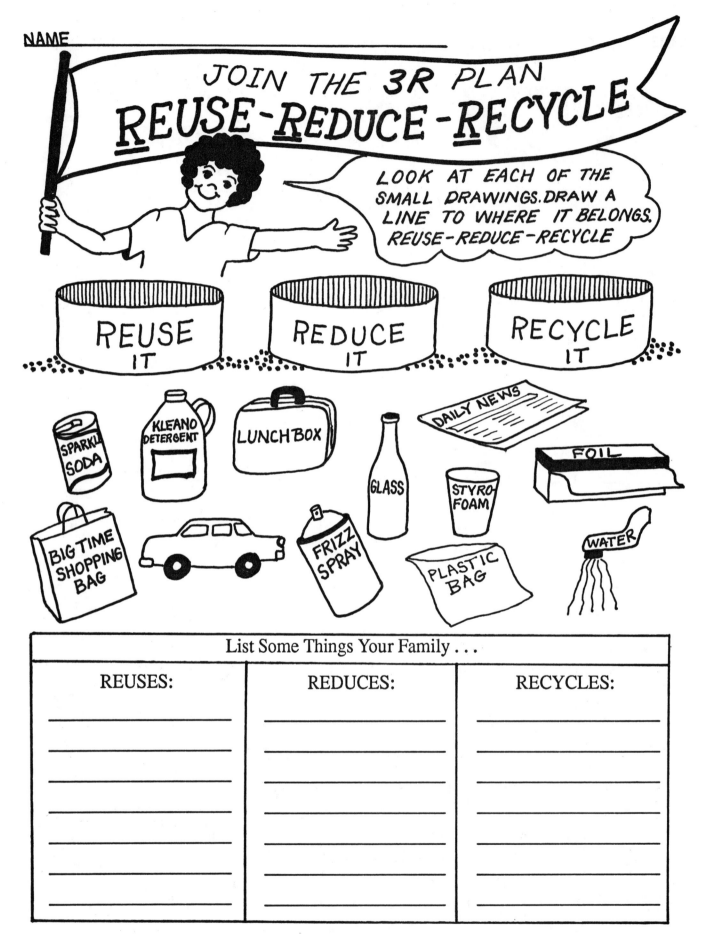

JOIN THE 3R PLAN
REUSE - REDUCE - RECYCLE

LOOK AT EACH OF THE SMALL DRAWINGS. DRAW A LINE TO WHERE IT BELONGS. REUSE - REDUCE - RECYCLE

REUSE IT   REDUCE IT   RECYCLE IT

SPARKL SODA — KLEANO DETERGENT — LUNCHBOX — DAILY NEWS — GLASS — STYRO-FOAM — FOIL — BIG TIME SHOPPING BAG — FRIZZ SPRAY — PLASTIC BAG — WATER

List Some Things Your Family . . .

REUSES:	REDUCES:	RECYCLES:

What Can We Do In The Classroom To Reuse And Recycle?

the FROG and the FLY

Finish the story.

The frog said, "I will eat you, fly."
The fly said, "Please don't eat me."
The frog said, "But I'm hungry."
The fly said, "So am I, let's go find
   some lunch."

_____
_____
_____
_____
_____
_____
_____
_____

What do you think frogs like to eat? _____

_____

TEAM NAME _____

MEMBERS _____

JOIN THE CLUB

While the population of our planet is increasing, problems of pollution are also increasing, while our natural resources are diminishing.

As a young person in today's society, *YOU* have a huge responsibility. You must be aware of existing problems, avoid potential problems, and take action. Don't be a "tag-along." Do your share!

TO DO:

1. Work together as a team.
2. Choose a team name.
3. Elect a secretary to take notes.
4. Select a regional "concern" from those in the box. (Or clear another with your teacher.)
5. Share what you know about the topic.
6. Do research to learn more.
7. Write a report together.
8. Write a letter to your congressman, newspaper, or an environmental organization. Explain your interest and find out what you can do.
9. Share your report with the class.
10. Have your secretary make out a conservation pledge for each team member.

CONCERNS

- Air pollution
- Water pollution
- Landfills
- Ocean dumping
- Natural resources
- Greenhouse effect
- Recycling
- Other?

THE CLUB — CONSERVATION PLEDGE

_____ has agreed to
         name
do his/her share to restore and maintain
a green, clean, and safe planet for
future generations.

date _____ secretary _____

NAME _____   NAME _____

A BEING WALK

A "Being Walk" is a special time to enjoy walking with a friend.

It's a time to celebrate nature, to examine leaves, to pick a wildflower, to look at insects or to listen to the birds. It's a quiet time.

Use this page to keep a log of your "Being Walk."

THESE ARE THINGS WE 👃

THESE ARE THINGS WE ✋

THESE ARE THINGS WE 👁

THESE ARE THINGS WE BROUGHT BACK.

THESE ARE THINGS WE 👂

Our walk was _____

_____

GOING, GOING, gone

Great dinosaurs once ruled the earth. They are now extinct. Animals have been vanishing from the earth since animals first appeared on the earth. Today, however, they are disappearing at a far greater rate than before. Many are in trouble. These are called "endangered species."

Why is this happening?

1. Destruction of Habitat
Humans are changing the natural environment needed by certain species. How? _____

_____

_____

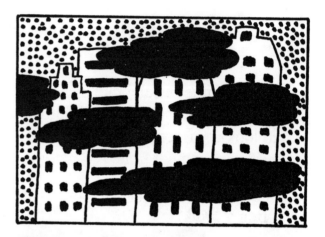

2. Killing of Wildlife
Commercial and sport hunters have played a major role in causing the extinction of wildlife. How? _____

_____

_____

TO DO: Take this page to your library.

Select one of the topics listed to the right and write a short report. Begin writing below and complete your report on the back of this sheet.

_____

_____

_____

_____

_____

– What is the worst threat to wildlife?

– Which species is in the most trouble?

– What is being done to save wildlife?

– How many kinds of animals are extinct?

– How can individuals help?

As the seasons change, so do their colors.

Make a color chart of the seasons. Follow the directions for the boxes.

In the A boxes put in the color—or colors—of that season.
In the B boxes write the color words.
In the C boxes make a seasonal symbol.
In the D boxes complete the sentence.

	FALL	WINTER	SPRING	SUMMER
A				
B				
C				

D	I like_____best, because_____ _____ _____

A HIKE IN THE WOODS

Read the story and fill in the blanks at the bottom of the page.

Tim and Jim were camping with their parents. After dinner one evening they decided to take a walk.

"Don't forget the safety rules," said Dad.

Mom added, "And don't stay out after dark."

"Okay, okay," replied both boys.

As they walked along, Tim said, "Let's go over the rules. I'll say them and leave out a word. You fill in the blanks."

"Sure," said Jim.

1. Don't pick _____.
2. Be careful with_____.
3. Always stay on the_____.
4. Never go_____.
5. Be careful around_____.
6. Never touch or taste strange_____.
7. Don't _____.
8. Never take _____.
9. Obey all _____.

FLOWERS AND PLANTS – CLIFFS – LITTER – CHANCES – ALONE – PLANTS OR BERRIES – TRAIL – FIRE – WATER – SAFETY RULES

Jim was great at giving all the right answers. He was a good camper and hiker.

Suddenly, Tim let out a yell and dropped his stick. He quickly climbed the nearest tree. His brother moved safely to the other side of the trail and began to laugh.

Tim had forgotten rule number ten. It was one of the most important safety rules. Do you know what it is?

_____

Answer: #10—Leave animals alone!

garden friends

Do you know there are many animals living in our gardens that are helpful to us?

Here's how some "friends" help us:

- Ladybugs eat plant lice.

- Sparrows eat grasshoppers and other insects.

- Praying Mantises eat insects that are bad for plants.

- Busy bees pollinate flowers.

- Lizards eat harmful insects.

- Earthworms make our soil rich by digging around and adding air.

- Frogs eat potato bugs, grasshoppers, slugs, and cutworms.

TO DO: Let's find a "garden friend."

1. Get a clean, empty jar with a lid.

2. Carefully cut holes in the top of the jar.

3. Add grass or leaves to the jar.

4. Look in your garden, schoolyard, or park for a "critter." (Please, no birds.)

5. Catch it carefully in your jar.

6. Cut out the label for your jar. Fill it out and tape it on.

7. Bring it to class to identify and share.

8. Return your garden friend to its home at the end of the day!

MY GARDEN FRIEND
is a_____
_____
I found it_____
_____
your name_____

just listen

The following Navajo Indian chant is several hundred years old. Try to memorize it.

"With beauty before me,
May I walk
With beauty behind me,
May I walk
With beauty above me,
May I walk
With beauty below me,
May I walk
With beauty all around me,
May I walk
Wandering on a trail of beauty,
Lively, I walk."

Now that you know this chant, go to a special place and walk quietly as the Navajo would. Think about the words, and enjoy the beauty.

When you return, write about what you saw and heard, what you felt and thought.

_____

_____

_____

_____

_____

_____

_____

_____

_____

_____

_____

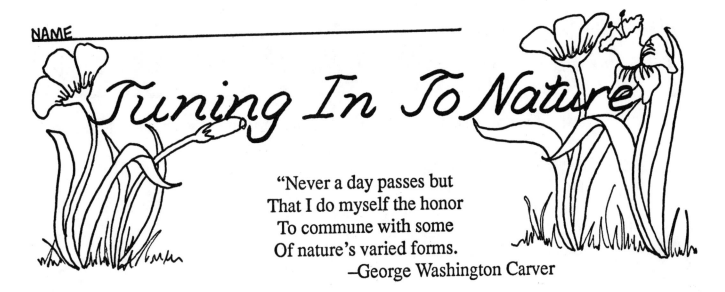

Tuning In To Nature

"Never a day passes but
That I do myself the honor
To commune with some
Of nature's varied forms.
—George Washington Carver

TO DO: Find a quiet place outdoors. Sit quietly for awhile. Take time to focus on some part of your environment. In the shape below, write about what you see and feel.

STOP time out

Time spent out of the classroom can be just the enrichment your students need. Take a day and leave the textbooks behind! You might:

—Expose your pupils to environmental waste and pollution.

—Share the wonders of natural settings.

—Reveal the excitement of museums, parks and gardens.

—Give them a "Living Experience!"

1.

2.

3.

4.

PLAN WELL! (Make some notes.)

1. Provide an orientation to build excitement. _____
_____
_____

2. Develop a careful plan to get the most out of your day. (Finances, bus, meals, timing, parents, guides, permission slips, rain gear, etc.) _____
_____
_____

3. Prepare a simple booklet for student notes and observations. You may suggest things to look for. (Keep it light and fun!) _____
_____
_____

4. Follow up with class discussions, stories, mural, pictures, and displays. Urge students to learn more about the place you visited. Encourage them to share the experiences with their families. _____
_____
_____

Where To Go?

—Conservation sites	—Forest rangers	—Fire stations
—Telephone companies	—Natural history museum	—Geologists
—Taxidermist	—Zoos	—Weather Forecasters
—Nurseries	—Planetariums	—Aquariums
—Hatcheries	—Utility Companies	—Parks, forests, farms

Emily's Garden

Bought some seeds
And took them home.
Put them deep
In dirt and loam.

Added water
(A little bit).
Pressed them down
And made them fit!

A few days passed,
I watched for green.
But nothing yet—
None to be seen.

What happened
To my tiny seeds?
Did I forget
One of their needs?

Let's see, I'll go
Down through my list,
And check how flowers
Must exist.

"Not too deep
And lots of sun."
Sure, I've done that
For every one!

Time's run out.
The seeds were bad!
I'll tell that store
I'm really mad!

I checked once more,
One misty morn.
No, it's too late—
Is all hope gone?

But look! They're here!
The earth did part,
And tiny plants
Have made a start.

They're green and fresh—
But fragile too.
I'll pull the weeds,
There's much to do.

I wondered as I
Knelt on the ground
At all the green
That's all around.

Did Mother Nature
Watch them all,
And help them grow up
Strong and tall?

And then I knew
What I did wrong.
It wasn't seeds
That took too long.

Of course, that's it!
It must be so,
That seeds—like kids—
Need time to grow.

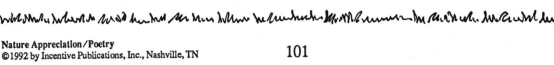

The Weatherman has a hard job. "Mother Nature" can be very unpredictable!

1. Check the weather each morning. (Use the TV, newspaper, radio, or sky.)
2. Write your prediction word on the calendar. (Don't forget to add the date.)
3. At the end of each day, check the weather.
4. If your word is correct, leave it alone.
5. If not, write a new weather word.

TORNADO	MON.	TUES.	WED.	THURS.	FRI.	SUNNY
ICY						FOGGY
RAIN						THUNDER LIGHTNING
PARTLY CLOUDY						CLOUDY
HOT						WINDY
COLD						HURRICANE

At the end of the month use your calendar to make a weather graph. How did you do as a weather predictor?

the Seal and the SeaLion

Seals and sea lions are mammals who need water as well as air. They have webbed flippers instead of paws or feet. Their bodies have heavy fur and are streamlined for easy swimming.

How are they different?

Sea lions have ear flaps and can turn their hind flippers forward.

Most seals lack ear flaps. Their rear flippers cannot be turned forward.

Seals and sea lions can be trained. We often see them playing ball at the aquarium. Polar bears and large sharks and whales will feed on them. But their greatest enemy is the human, who hunts them for their fur, oil, and meat.
THEY NEED OUR PROTECTION.

TO DO: Follow the dots to find out if this is a seal or a sea lion.

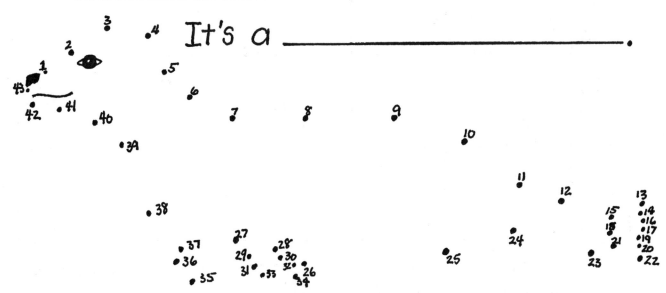

It's a _____.

I SEE IT
I LIKE IT
I NEED IT

When we look closely at our environment we can find things we don't always notice.

Think about (or go out and look at) your environment. Group the things that you see, smell, or hear into three groups. Write them in the symbols below. We've done one for you.

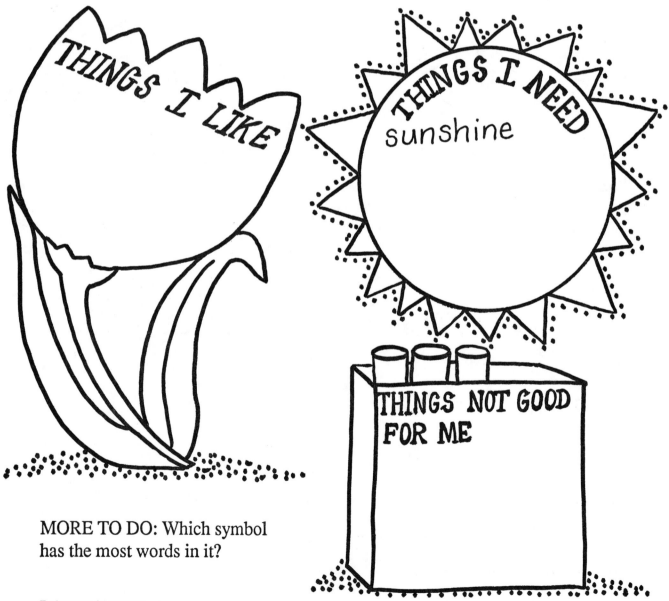

THINGS I LIKE

THINGS I NEED

sunshine

THINGS NOT GOOD FOR ME

MORE TO DO: Which symbol has the most words in it?

NAME _____

"WE CARE" CHECKLIST

Help To Make The Right Things Happen In Your World.

Draw a line from each sentence to one of the illustrations. Show if it's a good thing to do, or a bad thing to do.

> Example:
> Always leave the lights and TV on

1. Turn water off while you brush teeth......X

2. Throw away old newspapers X

3. Use lots of chemicals on your lawn........X

4. Use cloth diapers for babies..................X

5. Plant a tree X

6. Take long showers X

7. Keep the heat turned very high..............X

8. Flush toilets only when necessary X

9. Throw away plastic containers X

How do *YOU* show you care?_____

_____

What more can you do? _____

_____

PERSONAL WEATHER OBSERVATION

Did you ever notice how your feelings are affected by the weather?
TO DO: Look at these weather shapes. How would you feel on each kind of day?
Write it like this.

When we know there is a tornado. ★A very scarey thing an alert, I take my pillow and a favorite toy and go to the basement with my parents. Then we wait.

Draw and write your
weather observation on
the back of this sheet.

BATS in the attic

BERTIE

We probably have more mistaken ideas about bats than about any other animal!

Some people use "bat boxes" to encourage bats to live in their yard. Bats will eat insects and may eliminate the need for chemical pest killers.

They may *look* weird, but . . .

- Bats do not get caught in your hair.
- There are no vampire bats in the U.S.
- Bats are not blind.
- Bats are not mean—they are shy.
- Bats rarely carry rabies.
- Bats are very helpful. (One bat can eat between 500 and 5,000 insects in one evening.

Bertie the bat
Sleeps all day.
At night she flies—
Goes out to play.

She looks for food,
Insects and mice.
She thinks that bugs
And mice taste nice.

Help us she does,
'Round garden and house.
Eats all the bugs
Then for dessert has a mouse.

For dinner she eats
A thousand or two.
And each bug she eats
Won't Bite You!

Bats have a bad image
We need to erase.
So that people will see
That bats, too, have a place.

Make up a bat poem.

Write your bat poem in this bat space.

NAME _____   NAME _____

NAME _____   NAME _____

Complete this page on your own, then share it with your group. Decide on the best answers together. Share these with the class.

TO DO: Read the sentence in each box. Choose a face and write its number next to the box. Complete a short explanation or paragraph.

___ We were walking in the woods when we came upon a campfire out of control . . .

___ Dad's friend lit a cigar . . .

___ We got to the top of the mountain and stopped to look at the view . . .

___ As we walked along the beach we came upon some dead fish . . .

WATER WATER EVERYWHERE

DEFINITION: "Desalinization" is the removal of salt from water. Sea water must be desalinized in order to make it fit for human consumption.

Fresh water has become a problem in many areas of our world. Fortunately, scientists have developed several ways to solve this problem. Try the following experiment at home, or observe as your teacher does it.

Step 1. Begin with three cups of water (you may use ocean, bay or tap water with salt added—taste the water to be sure it is salty).

Step 2. Pour the water into a teakettle.

Step 3. Boil the water.

Step 4. Watch as the water vapor comes out of the spout.

Step 5. Using a pot holder, hold a pot lid above the spout.

Step 6. Catch the water drops from the bottom of the lid and let them drop into a pie pan.

Step 7. Taste the water.

What do you think has happened? _____

_____

Use your library to learn more about "Desalinization."

WHAT'S ON YOUR MIND?

**Respecting And Protecting Our Once Beautiful Planet
Is Everyone's Concern.**

TO DO: Make a statement about each item on the list below. Check the topics about which you want to find out more.

____ Air Pollution _____

____ Tropical Rain Forests_____

____ Recycling_____

____ Endangered Animals _____

____ Ozone Layer _____

____ Polluted Waters _____

____ Trash Disposal_____

____ Toxic Chemicals _____

____ Depleting Natural Resources_____

____ Your Concern_____

Choose one topic to find out more about. Do some research! Begin your report on the back of this sheet.

NAME _____

THE AIR WE BREATHE
IS IT CLEAN? IS IT SAFE? HOW DOES IT SMELL?

With the growth of our country came air pollution. The pure air of one hundred years ago is now mixed with smoke, soot, dust, gases, and chemicals.

Let's see how much you know. Read a question, then look for the correct answer on the right. Write it in the blank. When you have finished, check your answers. *DON'T PEEK!*

1. Indoor pollution can be caused by_____ _____.

2. Fireplaces and wood stoves cause_____ _____, which pollute the environment.

3. Pollution can _____the growth of crops and flowers.

4. Most pollution is caused by_____ _____.

5. Years of pollution can damage your_____.

6. The_____ from factories cause pollution.

7. Long term exposure to air pollution causes diseases such as _____.

8. _____ rots and soils things such as outdoor furniture and flags.

A. Stunt
B. Burning fuel
C. Health
D. Emphysema and bronchitis
E. Waste products
F. Smoke and ash
G. Natural gas, kerosene, and cigarette smoke
H. Polluted air

👁 👁 DON'T PEEK!
6–E; 7–D; 8–H.
3–A; 4–B; 5–C;
Answers: 1–G; 2–F;

MORE TO DO: Write a "Right To Clean Air" slogan. Cut it out. Take it home to hang on your refrigerator.

NAME

Chapter 5. GOOD AS GOLD BULLETIN BOARDS

Teachers often ask, "How long should I keep up a bulletin board ?" Our response is always the same. Take it down one day before your students lose interest.

Have you ever walked into a classroom that has tired bulletin boards? You can recognize them easily by their faded backings and their missing letters. Their papers have curled edges and are dated six months ago. A bulletin board like this is definitely a "has-been"!

A fresh, stimulating bulletin board breathes excitement into the classroom. It's a good indication that there's a lot going on!

"But they take too much time!" you say.

Not necessarily so! Learn to make quickie letters; have kids help put up the backing and make cutouts or illustrations. Remember, you are not entering an art contest, and the only individuals you aim to please are your students!

Display your students' work—provoke their interest. Make "working" boards that provide materials and information for a unit of study, skills to learn, or a worthwhile free-time project to make or think about.

There are those who consider making bulletin boards a "nuisance." However, if we were to give a one-word definition of a good bulletin board, it would be "stimulation." In this chapter we've provided fifteen suggestions, some of which are open-ended. The content you teach may not fit into the subject matter we show. That's okay—adapt them to your needs.

Keep your bulletin boards interesting to look at and appealing to use. Make them "happy boards" that add "pizzaz" to your classroom!

GOOD AS GOLD
BULLETIN BOARDS

E-Z LETTERING

You can be a "Letter-Making Whiz" in two easy lessons!

YOU WILL NEED: Scissors, pencil, felt tip markers.

Casual block lettering with a marker is fast and can be applied directly to your bulletin board. (Note: this technique should not be used with primary students as the letters may look confusing.)

LESSON ONE:

1. Use a pencil and lightly write the word you want in caps.
2. Go back and block out the letters, leaving the left side hidden.
3. When you are satisfied with the look, go over the letter with a marker. (Use the side for a broader look.)
4. Do it loosely—try not to be stiff and precise!

NOW LET'S PRACTICE

FOLD & CUT

This process is fast; even kids can learn it! Cut-out letters add pizzaz to your bulletin boards!

You can mass-produce letters by pre-cutting the size needed from construction paper. For practice, we suggest using standard sheets cut in quarters.

LESSON TWO:

1. Look at each letter of the alphabet. You will be cutting away the negative area.
2. When letters are symmetrical, fold paper horizontally or vertically.
3. Check the chart and make an alphabet.
4. Happy snipping!

115

PURPOSE:

To provide a place for monthly holiday happenings and thoughts. Make each month a special event!

CONSTRUCTION:

A good non-fading color should be used as background for this on-going bulletin board. Avoid wallpaper prints. You don't want a "busy board!" Make fun letters and change the calendar style for each month. Make a year's supply of "cakes" to note every student's birthday.

USE:

Encourage students to take part in the monthly preparation. Let them help with cutouts, listing events, etc. You may want to assign a special committee for each month. Use the board as a focal point for language and social studies lessons.

FOLD~A~CLOWN

John the Clown
Clowns are fun
At circus and parade.
They make me laugh,
But I am not afraid!

This one is silly,
His name is John.
I've put him to work
As a write-upon.

PROCESS:

Prefold 9" x 5" pieces of construction paper into about eight accordion folds. Have students copy a "fun" story or poem onto the folded paper. Assorted scraps of colored paper should be added to form body parts. You may want to provide pre-cut pieces to simplify the process.

A larger clown can be used as a focal point for the bulletin board.

• • •

A bright, happy way to display creative—or first—writing projects.

PURPOSE:

An old-fashioned movie marquee will add interest to a lesson on summarizing or writing reviews. A corridor is a good place for this interesting display. Crowds will gather!

CONSTRUCTION:

Add glitter, stars, and tinsel to a black background. Mount student work and pictures so they stand out. Make this a five star ★★★★★ bulletin board!

USE:

Give students a choice to add to this language arts display. Assign a movie or TV review. Discuss the rating scale so they can rank what they have seen. Change reviews every few days until all have been featured.

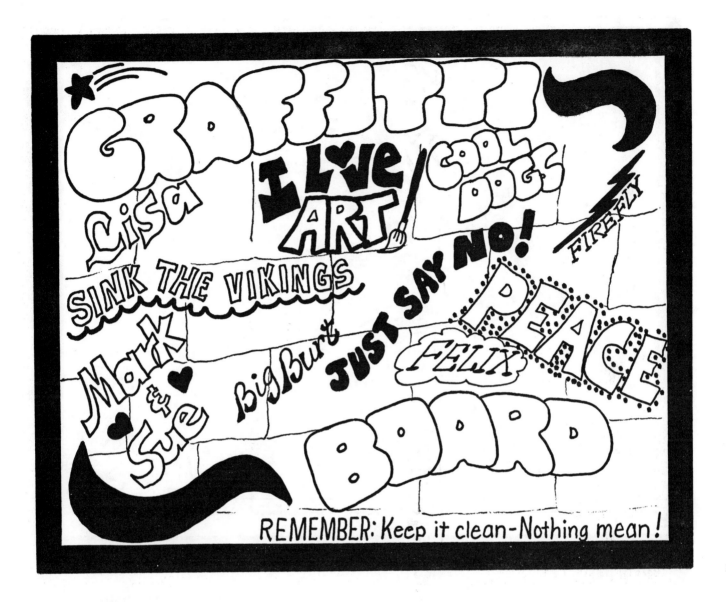

PURPOSE:

To provide students with a place to display their feelings, protests, anger, creativity, or frustration.

CONSTRUCTION:

Make a "brick wall" by using old wallpaper or painting white lines on red construction paper. Allow students to write on the backing, or on a separate piece of paper. Provide class time to add to the board. If space is limited, allow one "opportunity" per student.

USE:

Discuss the positive and negative aspects of graffiti. Where and why does it happen? Use this as an outlet for your student's creativity to let their voices be heard.

119

PURPOSE:
To make your students aware of the needy, and to foster a desire to help.

CONSTRUCTION:
- Draw and cut out two huge hands on which to put the title of this bulletin board.
- Ask students to bring in news clippings pertaining to global and local disasters, children or countries in need, or a local family in crisis.
- Post clippings and photos on the board.
- Have each child trace a hand and cut it out. Ask them to write on it, telling how they have helped someone in need. (Little things are okay.)

USE:
Discuss "reaching out" to others and share the stories. Your students may want to raise or collect money for a charitable fund. (See Chapter Seven for listings of non-profit organizations.)

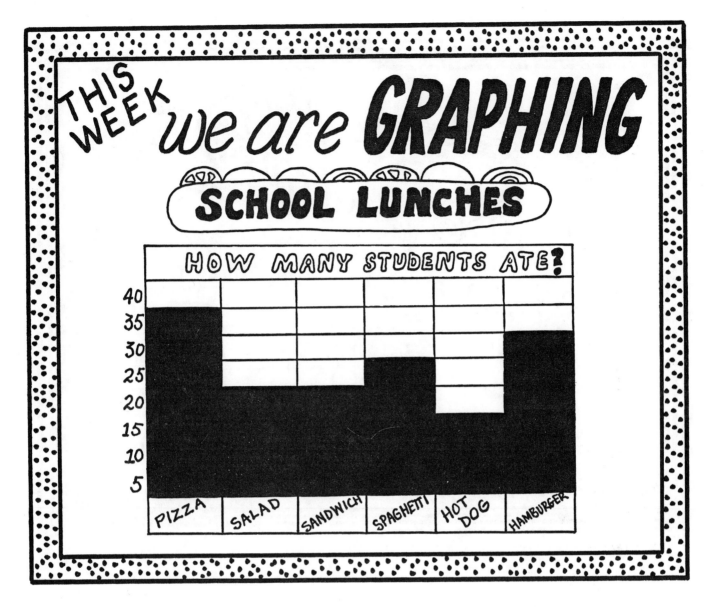

PURPOSE:

To provide a vehicle for collecting specific information, and displaying it visually. Reinforcing the concept of graphing.

CONSTRUCTION:

- Your background and lettering should stay up for as long as you will be teaching graphing.
- Change the graph topic weekly.
- Allow space on the sides for student graphs.

USE:

Representation by graphing is a creative way to show mathematical concepts such as fractions. Student interest will grow each week as a new topic is introduced. Make one giant class graph. Let the students help to decide the topic for the next graph!

121

PURPOSE:

To provide a cheerful "Back To School" welcome and a good way to review students' names and name spellings.

CONSTRUCTION:

- Cut and paste together large back-to-school items (pencil, eraser, book, book pack, lunchbox, etc.). Give them happy faces!
- Make a pocket chart large enough to hold a name card for each student. Tack it to the board.
- Write each child's name on the top half of a name card. Place the cards in the pockets.

USE:

As you take your first attendance, provide time for each student to take his or her card from the pocket. You may let them personalize cards with decorations. Use the chart for language activities—point out beginning sounds, letters, etc.

Name cards can be helpful for grouping activities, for taking attendance, and for substitute teachers.

PURPOSE:
To provide a stimulating display and process for independent student work or skill development.

CONSTRUCTION:
- Cover board with blue paper.
- Have students assist in constructing a large construction-paper rocket ship for the display.
- Attach numbered book pockets.
- Cut out small rocket ships to fit in the book pockets.

USE:
This multi-skill bulletin board may be used in all areas of the curriculum. The small rockets can provide math facts or problems, language area assignments, etc. A great way to provide for independent study.

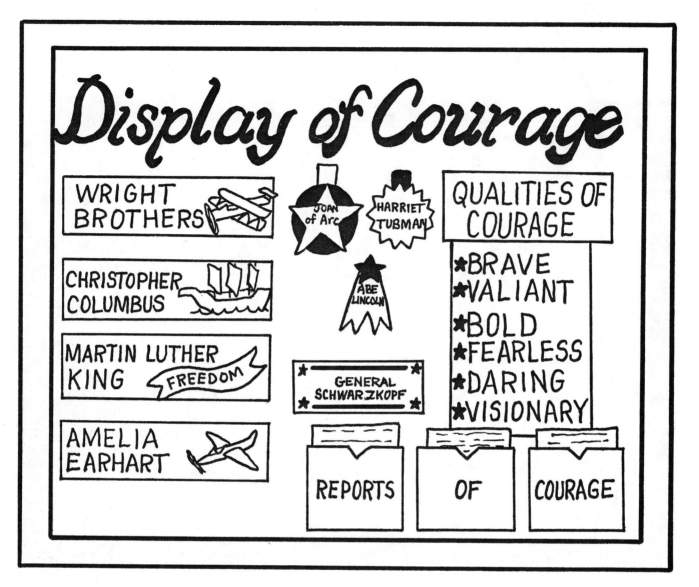

PURPOSE:

To provide stimuli and a vehicle for displaying research projects.

CONSTRUCTION:

- Write names of well-known historical figures. Add a simple drawing relating to each one.
- Add several report pockets for student work.
- Tack on student-made medals for each report.

USE:

Discuss the concept of courage and the qualities involved. With your class, make a list of heroes, people of great courage. Ask each student to research a person of choice and write a report telling of his or her bravery. The student should then design a medal for that person and add it to the display. Keep reports in the pockets for sharing.

DISPLAY BOARDS

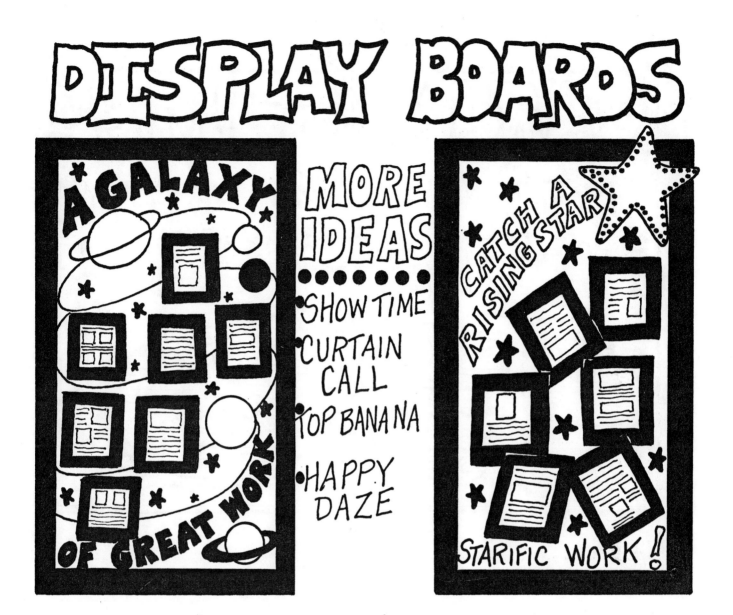

PURPOSE:

To provide a place of pride where work well done can be displayed. This is **NOT** merely a "space filler!"

CONSTRUCTION:

- Sky-blue backing is appropriate for both boards.
- Use lots of stars and glitter to add excitement.
- Mount or frame student work with contrasting colors.
- Try to show work completed by all students.

USE:

Small bulletin boards make good areas to display student work. A "glitzy" theme adds to the interest! Change the papers often; never let them get old and faded. Use this as a resource to give your students a "pat on the back."

PURPOSE:
To provide an eye-opening area for displaying biographies.

CONSTRUCTION:
- Use a brightly-colored backing.
- Make large primary letters.
- Decorate with party goods—hats, horns, balloons, streamers, etc. The gaudier the better!
- Pre-cut birthday cakes will fill the board.
- Student-decorated cake tops add to the party theme.

USE:
Pair students to write brief biographies of each other. Give time for an interview, note-taking, and writing. Provide each student with a simple cake on which to re-write the biography. The top of each cake can be decorated as a fancy showpiece!

Primary students can write simple sentences using words from a large word list. You may want to celebrate this activity with a real or mock party!

PURPOSE:

To provide an exciting theme for a "working" bulletin board.

CONSTRUCTION:

- Use a "watery" blue background.
- Add occasional swells or waves.
- Simple cutouts can create the "island scene."
- Sprinkle bold letters with glitter to make a "treasure" effect.
- Fold standard-sized brown construction paper in half. Use black markers to create the look of a treasure chest.

USE:

Each "floating" treasure chest can be "opened" to find a skill, message, or assignment for any curriculum area you are teaching. Students will enjoy opening the chests to see what is inside. You may want to number the chests to keep track of the activities. Chests may also be used to contain student written poems or creative activity.

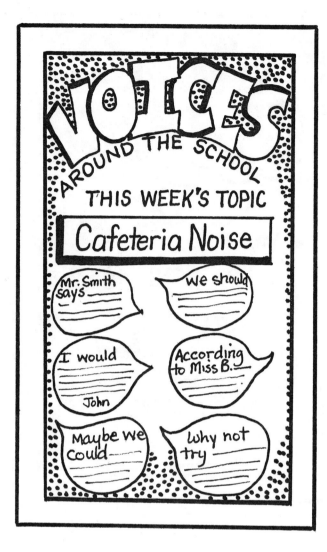

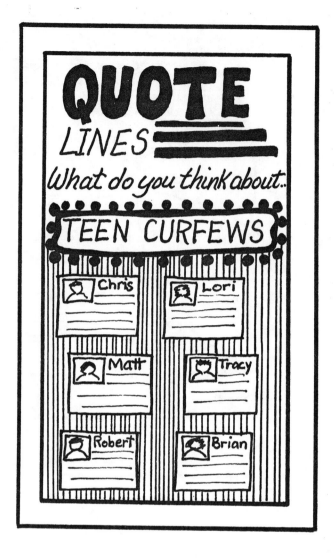

PURPOSE:

To provide a visual center where people can be "heard."

CONSTRUCTION:

- Use small bulletin boards in prime locations (corridors, lunchroom, foyer, etc.).
- Change topics weekly to avoid loss of interest.
- Write statements on white talking balloons for "voices."
- A current snapshot or polaroid picture should accompany the response to the question on "quotelines."

USE:

Teach a unit on interviewing and reporting. Give students assignments and have them report their findings. This is a great way to respond to school happenings or world events. Be sure to involve the whole school.

Chapter 6
14-KARAT IDEAS FOR THE ARTS

"The Arts" are sometimes thought of as "icing on the cake." Needless to say, teaching basic skills is of the utmost importance. However, without the accompaniment of art, music, drama, dance, and other such creative pursuits, school—and life—would lose its pleasure. For most people, there would be no thrill, enhancement, or gratification.

Here we have provided a short, simple play for your class to complete and then act out. We hope the play production page will simplify the tedious job of assigning roles and making sure *everyone* is contributing to the production. This can be a great way to learn about responsibility and cooperation.

"Make believe" is an important element of childhood (and is still inherent in much of what older children read and enjoy in movies or TV). Puppetry, mime, finger play, and creative movement all fit into this category. We have included pages to help you explore these areas.

We know that not everyone is "crafty," so you'll find some easy-to-do ideas for gift-giving—some just for fun!

We strongly believe that in these hectic times, we must *make* time for enrichment—for the things we *know* are worthwhile. These are the joyous pursuits that will add the "zest for life" to your classroom!

14 KARAT IDEAS
(The Arts)

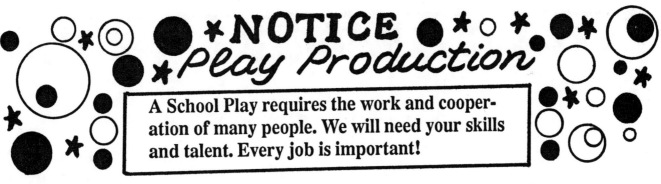

*NOTICE
Play Production

A School Play requires the work and cooperation of many people. We will need your skills and talent. Every job is important!

1. Director *(Directs the play and performance)*_____
_____

2. Producer(s) *(Organizes the work)* _____
_____

3. Stage Manager *(Gives cues, arranges scenery)*_____
_____

4. Scene Designer(s) *(Decides what props are needed)* _____
_____

5. Carpenters *(Build the props and scenery)* _____
_____

6. Artists *(Paint the scenery)* _____
_____

7. Costume Designer(s) *(Decides what is to be worn)* _____
_____

8. Makeup Artist(s) *(Applies makeup to actors' and actresses' faces)*_____
_____

9. Sound Technicians *(Make sound effects)*_____
_____

10. Prompter *(Helps performers who forget their lines)* _____
_____

11. Actors/Actresses *(Perform in the play)*

_____
_____
_____
_____
_____
_____

TRYOUTS TO BE HELD...
_____
at_____

THE SPOOKIEST GHOST

ACT I

This play takes place on Halloween Day, in a small country town.

Scene 1: *Sally Jones and her two brothers Todd and Kirk are walking home from school discussing the Halloween party to be held at the community center that evening.*

TODD: I don't know why you don't want to go tonight, Kirk. It's going to be neat.

SALLY *(shaking her head):* Yeah, Kirk. Everyone's going.

KIRK *(kicking a stone):* That's sissy stuff. Besides, I don't have a costume. I don't like costumes. They're dumb.

SALLY: But they're fun. Especially on Halloween. Mom and Dad are even dressing up tonight. They're going down the street to a party at the Taylors' house.

KIRK *(stops walking):* Really? I didn't know that grownups did that silly stuff, too.

TODD *(nods his head):* You bet they do. They do lots of silly stuff, but we're the ones who are always called "childish and silly."

SALLY: I know. When I try to act "old," Mom tells me "You're only ten years old." Then at other times she tells me to "grow up." Parents are very confusing at times! *(The two brothers stop walking and look at her. They nod their heads, then continue to walk. They kick leaves as they walk.)*

KIRK: Well, if everyone in the house is going somewhere, guess I'll go. I suppose the guys will be there. They always go where there's free food.

SALLY *(clapping her hands):* Great, Kirk! Mom and I can get a costume together for you.

KIRK *(shouts loudly):* No costume! That's definite!

Scene 2: *At home in the living room. Mom and Sally are draping Kirk with a sheet. Dad and Todd are in the background laughing.*

MOTHER *(kneeling on the floor in front of Kirk):* Stand still another minute and this will be fine. I'll just cut this off so you won't trip.

KIRK: But Mom, why won't anyone listen to me? I don't want to wear a costume. Especially this dumb thing. *(He waves his arms around in the air.)*

SALLY *(standing, holding a pincushion, giggles):* Oh, Kirk, you'll be great. No one will know you.

KIRK: Oh, yeah? Well, I'm going to wear my baseball cap. They'll know me, all right. *(He puts a cap on his head.)*

DAD *(taking baseball cap):* Now son, don't ruin it! You are a great ghost and your Mom and Sal did a good job. Be a sport.

KIRK *(groans loudly):* No one in this family listens! I'm always the one who's supposed to be a good sport!

THE SPOOKIEST GHOST (continued)

TODD (*walking around Kirk admiringly*): I think you look great, kid. Not as good as I do, of course. (*He flashes the pirate sword through the air and smooths his beard.*)

SALLY (*slinking around in her cat costume*): I don't look bad, either.

MOTHER: Okay, kids—if you are going to walk, you'd better get started. Your Dad and I have to get ready now, and it will take some time for me to get your father into his old tuxedo.

KIRK: Hate to miss that! But let's not prolong this! Hey, Sally, can I borrow these glow-in-the-dark bracelets of yours? They will look eerie!

SALLY: Anything to make you happy!

ACT II

Scene 1: *Sally and her two brothers are walking to the party. They carry flashlights and shine them around as they pass the cemetery.*

SALLY: Glad I know this cemetery well or I'd be scared. (*She waves her light.*)

KIRK: Why's that?

SALLY: Well, you know. It's Halloween and all.

TODD (*laughing*): Oh, Sal, that's silly. You know there's nothing to be afraid of— even on Halloween.

SALLY: I know it, but . . . (*She shines the light around from side to side.*)

KIRK (*makes a loud noise*): I'll scare 'em. BOO!

   (*Unseen by Sally, Todd and Kirk, two ghosts lean against a nearby tombstone.*)

GHOST 1: Dig that kid pretending to be a ghost. Do you know him?

GHOST 2: Yeah, he looks familiar to me.

GHOST 1: I see him around here once in a while. He does look spooky!

GHOST 2: I like those bright things he has on his arms.

GHOST 1: If we had those, we'd be the best-looking ghosts in the cemetery.

GHOST 2: Let's follow them. Maybe we can find out how to get some.

GHOST 1: Well, don't ask him. You'll scare him away. Most people don't know we're friendly.

GHOST 2: Okay. Let's go. (*Both ghosts wave their arms and begin to follow.*)

Scene 2: *At the door of the community center.*

HOBO 1: Hi, there! Who are you? Looks like Sally and Todd Jones with a "friend." (*He gives a loud laugh.*)

HOBO 2: Look—here come two more ghosts. Boy, their costumes look real. Come on in, guys. The party has just started.

WHAT HAPPENED NEXT?
(Finish writing the play.)

THE TRASHMAN

Make paper loop. Glue on back of puppet. Slip on finger.

KEITH THE TRASHMAN

A trashman's
What I want to be.
Of all the jobs,
It's the one for me.

I'll drive the truck
From street to street.
And pick through trash
That's often "neat."

I'd find old toys,
A game, a ball
That hardly has
Been used at all.

My Mom is always
Tossin' stuff.
She says, "Now, Keith,
You've got enough!"

Joe lets me lift
The trashcan lids.
He's nice to me
And other kids.

I like the job—
Don't mind the smell.
'Cause being trashman
Sure is swell!

"Make Believe" is an
important element of
childhood. Preserve it
in your classroom.

Excitement and creativity become
contagious when turning poems or
stories into plays and acting them out.
All students love pantomime, puppetry,
and finger play. The quiet child comes
alive when speaking through the voice
of another. You can extend and
reinforce many language skills by
providing time for "Let's Pretend."

• Read the poem "Keith The Trashman"
  and have students act it out.
• Have students pantomime workers
  they would like to be when they grow
  up. Make a list.
• Make a trashman finger puppet to go
  with the poem.

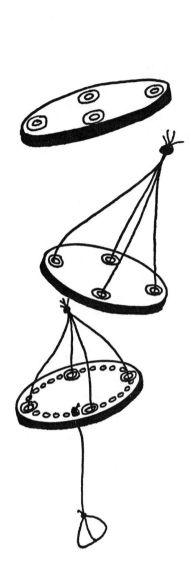

Four Winds

"The breeze will blow its freshness,
and the tinkling sound of wind chimes
will remind you of its presence."

Gather together: 1 plastic coffee can lid, ruler, hole punch, string, 20 items that will "chime" (i.e., small shells, spoons, keys)

DO THIS:
1. Punch four holes in the coffee can lid. Circle these holes with a marker.
2. Cut four pieces of yarn or string, each twenty-five inches long.
3. Knot each piece of string through one of the holes.
4. Pull the four strings together and knot them together a few inches from the top.
5. Punch five holes around the edge between each of the holes with the string.
6. Cut twenty pieces of string about ten inches long (you may vary lengths).
7. Attach one piece of string to each of the twenty holes.
8. Tie one "chime" to each length of string.
9. Hang up to catch the four winds!

FANTASTIC FOSSILS

Fossils have endured the ages. Ninety-million-year-old vertebrates can still clearly be seen, embedded in the sands of time.

Make your own contemporary fossil.

You will need:
- Fine beach sand or plasticene clay
- Object or shape with which to make the "fossil" (leaf, stick, stone, shell, etc.)
- Cake or pie pan
- Plaster of paris
- Box lid or shallow, flatbottom bowl to use for mixing plaster of paris

Process:
1. Press one stick of plasticene clay or two inches of beach sand in the bottom of the pan. (A thick "fossil" needs a deeper base.)
2. Smooth the surface.
3. Firmly press your selected object into the bottom of the pan. This will make an impression.
4. Carefully remove the object.
5. Make plaster:
   - (a) Fill a bowl up halfway with water.
   - (b) Pour plaster into the bowl until it forms a peak above the water.
   - (c) Stir until mixed.
6. Pour the mixture into the pan.
7. Let the plaster dry. (For hanging purposes, you can insert a piece of twisted wire before drying.)
8. Remove plaster "fossil."
9. You may want to paint the "fossil" with tempera paint. For a natural look, wipe off the excess paint before drying.

Memory Plates

Special people, places, and occasions are often pictured on a "commemorative plate." We hang these with pride.

The word "commemorate" means to celebrate or honor.

Who are some people you are proud of? _____

_____

What occasions will you always remember? _____

_____What are some places you will never forget?

_____

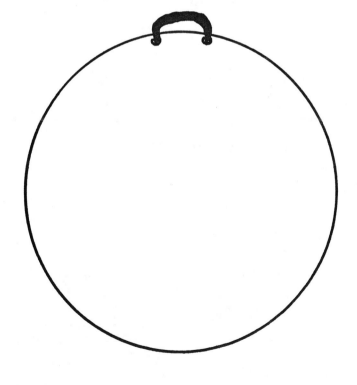

You will need:
- Paper plate
- Markers or crayons
- Hole punch
- Yarn

Construction:
1. Decide what you want to draw on your memory plate.
2. Make a rough drawing in the circle.
3. Transfer the drawing to the paper plate.
4. On the back, write what this place "commemorates."
5. Punch holes and add yarn for hanging.
6. Give to someone, or hang in your room.

Remarkable Recycling

Litter Catch

A waxed milk carton can quickly be turned into a container for litter.

Here's how:

Completely open the top of a quart or half-gallon carton. Cut around the top, leaving one side. Cut a hole for hanging. Glue on colorful pictures from magazines and apply varnish.

Rocket Toss (or Catch) Game

You can toss it high, or play catch with a partner.

Here's how:

Cut a plastic detergent bottle in half. Leave the cap on to give it weight. Decorate this "rocket cone" with a permanent marker.

Cut a six-inch-wide strip of the Sunday comics for color. Make the strip long enough to wrap around the bottle a few times. Tape it around the bottom edge of the bottle, then cut it into thin strips to "fringe" it.

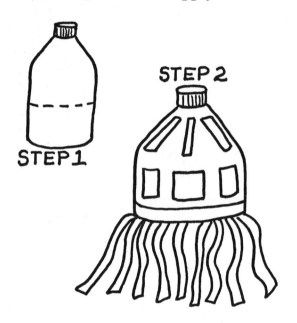

Take-Along Totes

A handy carrier to take to a "shut-in"!

Here's how:

Use a six-pack soft drink carrier, or an empty cereal box with the top cut off. Cover the container with wallpaper, construction paper, or self-adhesive paper. Reinforce the edges with tape. You may personalize the tote with cut-outs or pictures. Add a braided-yarn handle to the cereal box.

MAKE IT-A GIFT HIT

Seasonal Letter or Napkin Holder

You will need:
- A medium-sized detergent bottle
- Construction paper
- Hot water   • Scissors

Construction:
1. Soak the plastic container in hot water to make it easier to cut.
2. Cut off the top half of the container.
3. Cut straight down from each side.
4. Cut out the middle section.
5. Shape the front and back by cutting each top into rounded shapes.
6. Glue on a seasonal shape, holiday message, etc.

Multi-Use Juice Cans

You will need:
- Washed-out frozen juice cans (with lids) • Pictures, old matchbox covers, photos, wallpaper, wrapping paper, etc. • Yarn or rickrack • Glue • Hammer and screwdriver

USES:
- BANK
- USED RAZOR BLADE CAN
- FLOWER VASE

Construction:
1. Cut slots in can lids. (Use hammer and screwdriver or ask custodian to help.)
2. Put lid back on the top of the can and tape around edge.
3. Add covering of choice to sides.
4. Add glue at seams, then cover with yarn or rickrack.

Non-Toxic Flower Arrangement

You will need:
- Round coffee filters
- Water
- Food coloring
- Pipe cleaners or baggie ties
- Plastic sheet or plastic bags

Construction:
1. Fold a coffee filter in half.
2. Fold in half again.
3. Sprinkle water on the filter.
4. Add drops of food coloring.
5. Place between plastic sheet to spread the color (make patterns).
6. Spread out to dry.
7. Re-fold filter and gather bottom with baggie tie.
8. Group to make a bouquet. These "flowers" can be poked into fruits for a centerpiece as they are non-toxic.

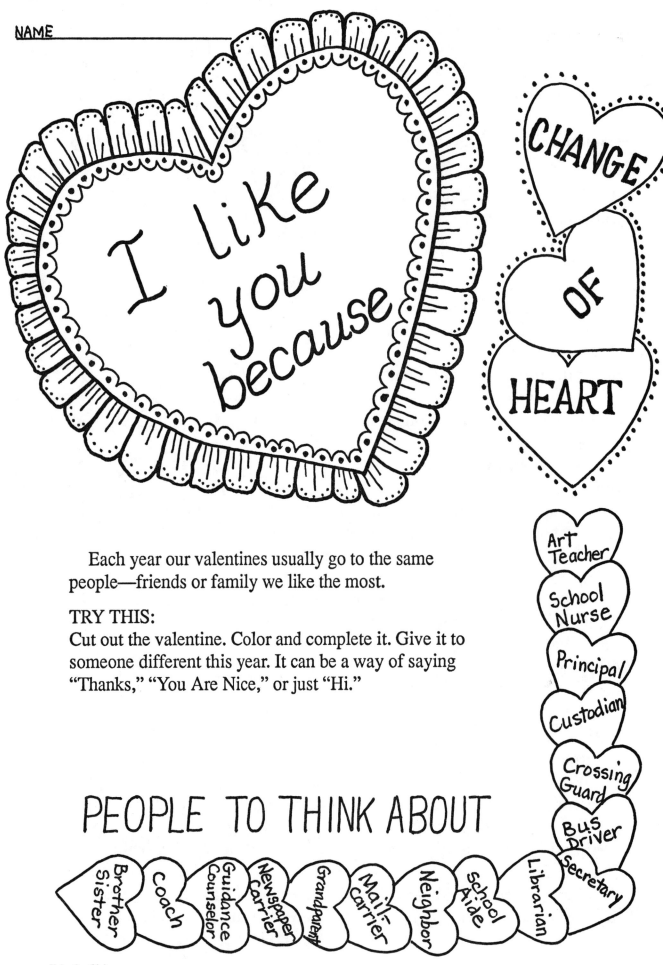

I like you because

CHANGE OF HEART

Each year our valentines usually go to the same people—friends or family we like the most.

TRY THIS:
Cut out the valentine. Color and complete it. Give it to someone different this year. It can be a way of saying "Thanks," "You Are Nice," or just "Hi."

PEOPLE TO THINK ABOUT

Art Teacher
School Nurse
Principal
Custodian
Crossing Guard
Bus Driver
Secretary
Librarian
School Aide
Neighbor
Mail Carrier
Grandparent
Newspaper Carrier
Guidance Counselor
Coach
Brother
Sister

My winter world
Is cold and white—
Frosty days
And dark, still nights.

To Make A Snowflake

You will need:
- One tablespoon salt mixed with one-fourth cup hot water
- White paper or newsprint
- Construction paper (blue)
- Scissors
- Ruler
- Paintbrush or cotton swab

Construction:
1. From white paper, cut a circle about seven inches in diameter.
2. Fold paper in half, then in thirds (Diagram "A").
3. Cut out snowflake design (Diagram "B").
4. Open paper to see a beautiful snowflake pattern.
5. Place snowflake on construction paper.
6. Use small pieces of tape in corners.
7. Use brush or swab to paint all openings with salt mixture.
8. Allow liquid to evaporate.
9. Remove pattern.

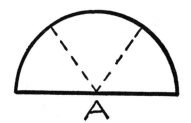

A

B

. . . The wondrous flakes
Begin to fly,
Like magic feathers
From the sky.

SEASON FOR GIVING

Take-Home Gifts For All Seasons

1. **Mitten Hanger:** *A Fun Gift To Make!*
   - Decorate a sturdy paper plate with a face (child, snowman, etc.).
   - Punch two holes in the bottom of the plate and reinforce with tape.
   - Slip yarn through the two holes and tie clothespins on ends.
   - Add another hole, and a loop of yarn at the top for easy hanging.

2. **Edible Wreaths:** *Catch The Spirit!*
   - Have each child bring in a corrugated box side.
   - Cut into "wreaths."
   - Paint the "wreath" or cover with a fabric.
   - Have pupils bring decorated cookies or bake them together.
   - Wrap cookies individually in clear plastic.
   - Tie them to the wreath with yarn or ribbon.
   - Add a bow.

3. **Holiday Simmer:** *An Aromatic Delight!*
   - One small reclosable plastic bag for each child.
   - Decorate with "scraps" and glitter.
   - Tape a student-made copy of Poem/Directions on each bag.
   - Add the "simmering" fragrance.
     Mix:
     - 1 tablespoon whole cloves
     - 3 sticks cinnamon
     - 1 teaspoon ground nutmeg
     - Dash of allspice
     - Orange peel (optional)

HOLIDAY SIMMER

This holiday simmer
Is nothing to eat.
It's a non-edible
seasonal treat.

Add 2 cups of water
To contents herein.
Simmer it slowly,
Let the season begin.

PUPPET THEATER

Early Childhood is a Time for Magic and Wonder.

Extend your language curriculum through the joys of puppetry!

- Construct a puppet stage using an old cardboard box. Paint a scene on the stage.
- Make simple hand puppets with fabric, paper, vinyl, socks, etc.
- Have students write poems or scripts to act out. Try this one:

SIMPLE HAND PUPPET

Cut 2 puppets from fabric. Glue together. Let dry completely before using.

WILLIE THE WEATHERMAN

Now Willie The Weatherman
Is here to say
The kind of weather
We'll have today.

Will it snow or sleet?
Be cold with showers?
Or will it rain
To help spring flowers?

The roads will be icy!
The day will be hot!
Oh dear, I don't know—
Weather or not!

Puppetry
©1992 by Incentive Publications, Inc., Nashville, TN

TIM *the friendly dragon*

This knight in shining armor
Stands straight and proud and tall.
He fights the fiery dragon,
Saving "fairest of them all."

One day there was a battle.
Tim the dragon fell.
He smoked and roared upon the ground,
Then a flower he did smell.

Now Marianne the Princess,
Could go her merry way.
Perhaps the knight so proud and tall
Would even want to stay?

She watched the silent dragon
Who held the flower tight.
He's not like other dragons—
He doesn't want to fight!

She cried, "Don't kill the monster,
I'll save him in the end.
He isn't mean or angry—
He just needs a friend."

The knight in shining armor
Let out a weary sigh.
He put away his shield and sword.
Tim held his flower high.

Now Marianne the Princess
Is still "fairest of them all."
Her knight in shining armor
Still stands proud and tall.

But Tim the big, green dragon,
Enjoys another life.
He tends their castle garden,
And even found a wife!

The children play and dance with Tim,
They wander by the stream.
He tells them tales of knights so bold,
And what makes dragons mean.

"I thought that no one loved me,
So I knew I had to scare!
I never had a loyal friend,
But now, I've learned to care."

Finger Puppet patterns can be
traced on posterboard,
then used to act out the poem.

Make paper loop. Glue on back of puppet. Slip on finger.

KNIGHT

MARIANNE

TIM

Chapter 7 · GOLDEN NUGGET STOCKPILE

The days slip by and there's much to do! It seems there is a never-ending mountain of work to correct, subjects to teach, tests to give, and students that need your help.

In this chapter we've provided some "helpers," simple ideas, time savers, and easy filler for those unexpected moments. There are a few classroom management suggestions that we think are "gems," and that work well in almost any situation.

We've included two pages that will help you reach out to parents. There are times when they, too, need a "lifesaver."

We think one of the most important pages is the "Pat On The Back." As you know, positive recognition and reinforcement are the most rewarding techniques of teaching. Kids thrive on them. So do teachers!

HEART OF GOLD ♡ AWARD

YOU ARE GREAT!

This certificate of achievement acknowledges your untiring effort to teach and help children grow.

GOLDEN NUGGET STOCKPILE
(Especially For The Teacher)

GOURMET CORNER

The following recipe card can be filled in, cut out and used at a specific gift-giving time.

- Make up a class list of appropriate words or terms (ingredients).
- Have students fill in the blanks on their recipe cards.
- Have students add color to their cards.
- Make envelopes and give the cards to loved ones.

RECIPE FOR FRIENDSHIP
1 C. Kindness
2 C. loyalty
1 C. cheerfulness
1 TBS. helpfulness
Sprinkle with LOVE

♥ RECIPE FOR _____

♥ FROM THE HEART OF _____

♥ 2 C. _____

♥ 1 C. _____

♥ 1½ C. _____

♥ 2 TBS. _____

♥ MIX TOGETHER AND _____

Everyone's doing it. Get into the act!

Make lots of copies of these "coupons" and give them to students when they deserve a bonus, treat, or reward.

When the word gets out, you'll be swamped with "good deeds"!

SUPER DUPER BONUS COUPON

TO _____

FOR _____

EXPIRATION DATE _____

Teacher's Initials

★★★ FANTASTIFICATE ★★★

FOR _____

AWARDED TO _____

BECAUSE _____

COUPON EXPIRES _____ _____

OFFICIAL SIGNATURE

FANTASTIC

UNDER THE HAMMER

A little time to spare? The art teacher just got sick . . . no recess . . . it's raining? Whatever the reason, here are some "fillers" that can be fun and relate to an area of the curriculum.

1. WORD ADDUP: Make an alphabet chart and assign a numerical value to each letter. (A=1; Z=26.) Place the chart where all students can see it. Read a sentence (or a word) to the class. Have them write it and then add the value of each letter. The first one to answer correctly gets a number of points that equals the sum of the numerals in the answer. You may want to divide the students into groups to ensure equal abilities.

2. ROUND ROBIN: Provide several "stations" at the chalkboard, and work simultaneously. One child writes a number; a second one adds a math symbol; a third adds a number and the equal sign; a fourth writes the answer. If the equation is correct, the children sit down and another group takes their place.

3. HOW MANY OF YOU?: Lead a "values voting" activity. Ask simple questions and have students show how they feel by responding with thumbs UP for "yes," thumbs DOWN for "no." Arms folded means "I'm not sure."

4. RAP TIME: Give a title or theme and ask students to write a "Rap." Provide time for those who want to present their raps.

5. SNAPPY STORY: Write a number of brief scenarios on 3 x 5 cards. Select topics of concern where choices must be made (social, school, family, environment issues). Have students volunteer to "role play" in front of the class, or divide them into small groups for decision-making.

Example: "Tom, Jack, and Susie were walking home from school one day. When they passed the ballfield they saw Joe, a kid they knew, hit a baseball and break a car window. Joe and his friend ran away." What happens next?

WHO NEEDS HELP?

Who Needs Help?

When a world crisis strikes, how can we help?
When your students look for information, to whom can they write?

HERE'S WHO CAN HELP (Relief Agencies)

American Red Cross
Box 37243
Washington, DC 20013

UNICEF
333 E. 38th St.
New York, NY 10016

Salvation Army
799 Bloomfield
Verona, NJ 07044

B'nai Brith International
1640 Rhode Island Ave. NW
Washington, DC 20036-3278

World Vision
919 W. Huntington
Monrovia, CA 91016

Save The Children
54 Wilton Road
Westport, CT 06881

American Friends Service
4th and Arch Streets
Philadelphia, PA 19106

Lutheran World Relief
390 Park Avenue
New York, NY 10016

World Concern
P. O. Box 33000
Seattle, WA 98133

Food For The Hungry
7729 E. Greenway Rd.
Scottsdale, AZ 85260

OXFAM America
115 Broadway
Boston, MA 02116

YMCA
101 N. Wacker Street
Chicago, IL 60606

HERE'S WHERE TO WRITE (Student Resources)

American Fisheries Society
1040 Washington Bldg.
Washington, DC 20005

Environmental Defense Fund
P. O. Drawer 740
Stony Brook, NY 11790

U. S. Fish & Wildlife
Washington, DC 20250

American Forestry Assn.
919 17th St. NW
Washington, DC 20006

National Geographic Society
17th and M Sts. NW
Washington, DC 20036

U. S. Weather Bureau
Washington, DC 20250

Animal Welfare Institute
P. O. Box 3492
Grand Central Station
New York, NY 10017

Sierra Club
1050 Mills Tower
San Francisco, CA 94104

Wilderness Society
729 15th St. NW
Washington, DC 20005

REMEMBER WHEN

Remember when
My hands were small?
But now I've grown,
I'm getting tall.

My prints were there
On walls and door.
But now they're clean—
I wash them more!

Here's one more print;
It's really neat.
I've left it here
right on this sheet.

Someday you'll say
"Look at this page,
How cute you were
At that young age."

You'll check me out—
Compare my size.
Say "How you've grown,
You're quite a prize!"

We both will smile,
You'll point, and say—
"That small child's hand
Was clean that day!"

handprint

_____
name

_____
date

151

SUMMER DATE BOOK

AUGUST

JUNE

JULY

Think About Doing

1. Look for bird feathers.
2. Make a scrapbook of leaves.
3. Look at the clouds; write a poem.
4. Dry some flowers.
5. Write your life story.
6. Visit an old or sick person.
7. Hunt for insect homes.
8. Pick some wildflowers.
9. Watch and identify some birds.
10. Clean the attic, garage, or your closet.
11. Read a book.
12. Bake something.

Fold page in half. Draw a design or special title on the front. Use back to list appointments.

A PAT ON THE BACK

We all thrive on positive reinforcement: chests puff out, eyes gleam, and a sigh of pleasure escapes. Don't forget how important this reinforcement is, and reward your students often. Watch them grow!

A HUGE SUCCESS

HUGS FOR YOU

PURR-FECT NEWS FOR HOME

TEACHER

gold dust

A Sprinkling of Ideas for the Young Student!

DIRECTION BOX: Make a collection of funny hats, sunglasses, clothing, toys, etc. • Write a 3 x 5 card direction for each item in the box. ("Put on the red sunglasses; wear the hat with the feather; put on the striped sock; hold the doll with the yellow hair; etc. . . .") • Assign small groups to use the box for a period of time. • Children take turns drawing a card, reading it aloud (help is okay), then following the direction. • There will be lots of giggles from silly-looking students!

PART READING: Find stories that have a lot of dialogue. • Divide your class into groups just large enough for one "part" each, plus a reader for non-dialogue. • Read the story aloud like a play. • You may want to group the readers on ability levels. • After practice, you may ask them to read to a lower grade.

COMIC CUT-UPS: Select a few Sunday comics your class likes and understands. • Cut apart the sections. • Mix them up. • Use a pin or tape to attach one section of a comic to the front of each student. • Have the students mill around the room until each one finds the rest of his or her group. • Have the students put themselves in order according to story sequence. They can read their comics to the class. • Important: Be sure that you have the correct number of comic sections for your students.

SHOW AND TELL (AND THINK): Show and Tell, a tried-and-true "oldie," can become an interdisciplinary teaching tool by doing some of the following:

—Assign an alphabet letter theme.

—Assign a color for the day.

—Assign a theme (hobby, science, nature, favorite food, toy, etc.).

—Give "talk back" time. Allow students to respond, starting with "I think . . ."

—Write a few sentences as a group. The sentences should pertain to that day's show-and-tell topics, i.e., "Sam had a good trip."

—Extend this activity into your Language Arts curriculum.

DEAR PARENT:

Summer vacation is almost upon us. For many of you, summer vacation is the time you hear, "What can I do now? I'm bored."

A growing number of parents work; all are busy at home. However, there are things you can do with your child to make the summer "pay off." Vacation from school can be more than putting in time until school starts in the fall. We all need a sense of purpose.

The following is a list of things you may encourage your child to do. Or—if time permits—do some of them together. If you are out of the house during the day, perhaps you can arrange for a "tell me about your day" time in the evening.

Places To Visit

1. Natural History museum
2. Art museum
3. Fish hatchery
4. Zoo
5. Planetarium
6. Artist studio
7. Cemetery
8. Pet store
9. Nursing home
10. Boat yard
11. Fire department
12. Aquarium
13. College campus
14. Farm
15. Plant nursery
16. Botanical garden

Things To Do Or Think About

1. Go on a picnic.
2. Take some pictures.
3. Play a game.
4. Water play.
5. Garden.
6. Bird watch.
7. Catch butterflies.
8. Walk in a stream.
9. Fly a kite.
10. Read a cereal box.
11. Help a sick person.
12. Exercise.
13. Clean the attic.
14. Visit Mom or Dad at work.
15. Make a scrapbook.
16. Camp out.

Have a wonderful summer together!

Sincerely,

SPECIAL days ways

Encourage your students to "reach out." It's a sure way to build character and make a positive impact on their future.

Visit A Nursing Home

Bring cookies; read a story; make cards or pictures; sing songs; push wheelchairs; visit; bring a pet. Play a game; polish fingernails; go for walks; adopt a grandparent. A visit will be appreciated.

Raise Money For A Class Cause

Think about a good cause—someone or some place that needs help. Think of ways to earn money. (Do odd jobs; cut lawns; weed gardens; wash cars; walk pets; babysit; have a garage sale; sell lemonade; have a bake sale; recycle scrap materials; sell magazines or candy bars.) It's important that the students *earn* the money, not merely collect it.

Clean-Up Time

Help with a community or school clean-up day. Pick up trash; recycle litter. If there is not a program—start one. Put up posters and advertise for help! Encourage a feeling of community pride, and working together for a cause.

Reading Program

Provide time for students to practice reading a special story, then visit a lower grade and have students read to small groups. If there is a school for the blind in your town, students can make tapes that can be used by blind children. Slower readers should be permitted to read also. They can read to one small child at a time until confidence is gained. Story-telling is a good technique for helping less able readers gain skill and confidence. Let them practice on each other until they are ready for an audience.

Cooperative Learning is an important element in today's education. Cooperation, leadership, trust, and communication are all tools that will enhance school climate and last a lifetime.

THE TOWN MEETING

When a decision or choice is to be made in your classroom, try a town meeting. In this democratic forum, everyone participates in decision making. Ideas, opinions, and suggestions can be offered by anyone.

- Choose a moderator who will be fair. This can be done by election or appointment.
- A secretary must take careful minutes so that a review of the meeting is available.
- Let your students run the meeting and let all voices be heard.
- A majority decision must be upheld by all. It is important to accept and respect the ideas of others.

CIRCLE OF LEARNING

- Divide your class into groups of four to six.
- Provide the groups with enough worksheets so that each student has one. Elect a group leader.
- Ask each student to read the information given on the worksheet, then answer the questions individually.
- Students will work as a group to discuss answers and decide on one group response for each question (group response may be a combination of individual responses).
- All group members' names will be placed on the final answer sheet.
- A group grade is given for the work. Each member receives the same grade.

HELP GROUP

Arrange your day so that approximately fifteen to thirty minutes can be used for "help" sessions.

- Post "help lists" and encourage students to sign up where needed.
  Example: "Today at 2:30 Mark will give help with fractions. Stacy will be helping with the homework assignment."
- Urge students who need the extra help to attend. Be sure no stigma is attached to this voluntary service.
- Remind your class that there will be times when everyone who wants to can teach or share something he or she does well.

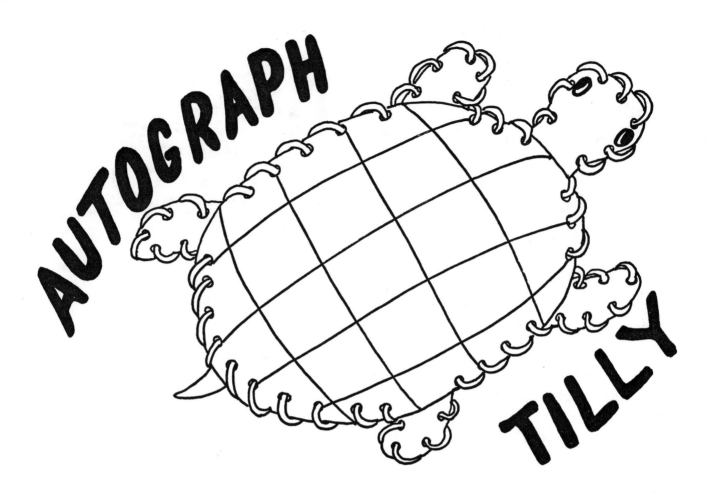

"Tilly" is Fun to Make and Fun to Use

You will need:
- Large sheets of "turtle-colored" construction paper
- Scissors
- Hole punch
- "Filler" (foam, tissue, shredded newspaper, etc.)
- Yarn
- Markers or crayons

Construction:
1. Pre-cut or trace construction paper turtles.
2. Give each student two turtle shapes.
3. Have students punch holes around the outer edges.
4. Have students lace the two parts together.
5. "Stuff" with "filler" when almost finished lacing.
6. Draw features and squares on both sides.
7. Use turtles for autograph "critters" at the end of the school year.